RONALD—
Ha! Ha!
Your turn!

3/98

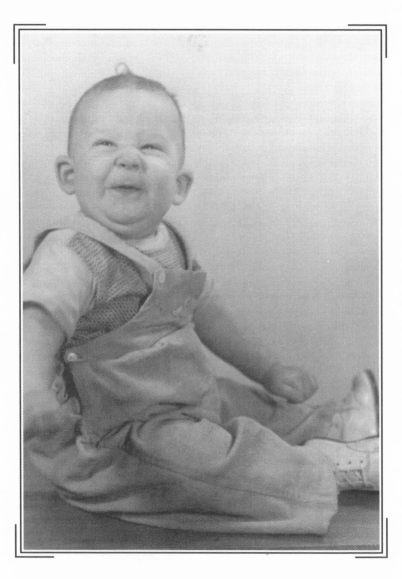

Look who's laughing!

Laughter Legacy

by DAVID GINN

derived in part from the comedy

notebooks of my funny friend, the late

GENE GORDON

A Scarlett Green Publication
Lilburn, Georgia USA

First Edition: February 1, 1998

Publisher's Cataloging in Publication
(Prepared by Quality Books Inc.)

Ginn, David
    Laughter legacy / by David Ginn
    p. cm.
    "Derived in part from the notebooks of my funny
friend, the late Gene Gordon."
    Includes index.

    ISBN: 0-9649318-2-6

    1. Wit and humor. 2. Public speaking. 3. Conjuring.
4. Gordon, Gene, 1903-1994. I. Gordon, Gene, 1903-
1994.   II. Title.

PN6162.G56 1996   808.88'2
                      QB195-20541

Table of Contents

Dedicated to the Memory of

GENE GORDON

magician, author, magic dealer,

funny talker, mentor and friend

It Matters To Me

IN SEPTEMBER 1994, I lost a good friend.

His name was Gene Gordon. He was a magician, comedian, magic dealer, funny talker, and author of *Gene Gordon's Magical Legacy,* one of the finest books ever written in the field of magic. He would have been 91 years old in October of that year.

In the early 1920's, Gene helped start a magic club, which he and Len Vintus boldly dubbed the International Brotherhood of Magicians. Over 70 years later, it's still going strong.

For twenty years, Gene worked school programs across the USA in the 1920's and 30's. In the 40's, 50's, and 60's he ran Gene Gordon's Magic Shop in Buffalo, New York, popularizing such magic tricks as Professor's Nightmare, Fraidy Cat Rabbit, and many Hen Fetsch effects until his retirement. I still have and proudly use my Gene Gordon model Fraidy Cat Rabbit.

In 1980, my wife Lynne and I both edited and published Gene's book of a lifetime. *Gene Gordon's Magical Legacy* became a landmark in magic and led to Gene being recognized with the 1981 Masters Fellowship Award from the Academy of Magical Arts in Hollywood, California.

David and Lynne Ginn with Gene Gordon, holding the famous mind-reading dog, Ridiculous Rupert, at NYCAN 1980 in Toronto.

From 1979 to 1990, Gene continued a friendly correspondence with Lynne and me, advising us how to raise daughter Autumn and giving us magical life advice. Often he would include little jokes and quips, just for the fun of it, sometimes typed on little slips of paper, sometimes news clippings. Many times he referred to his comedy notebooks he had been keeping for forty years or more, but I never actually saw them.

Then, a few months after Gene's death, his wife Ruth called me to ask if I wanted "the notebooks."

Naturally, I said yes, assuming these "notebooks" consisted primarily of material we had used in Gene's book fourteen years earlier.

The Notebooks

One week later, here came the weathered, wire-bound notebooks, worn with age, each hand-written with a dozen different pens, from fountain pens to ball points, even some entries inscribed in pencil.

One night I started reading this huge assortment of one-liners, jokes, thoughts, and sayings. I was surprised to discover that only a few of the lines from *Magical Legacy* were in these pages. Instead, I found dozens of lines per page, over a hundred pages in all, none of which I had ever heard—*and most of which I thought were funny!*

My original idea was to include these gags in a huge patter book I started in 1986, as yet unpublished. Then I thought about categorizing these lines and putting them out as a Gene Gordon patter book. I called Ruth and asked her opinion. Here is what she said on the telephone and later put into writing:

Gene wrote his book, *Gene Gordon's Magical Legacy*, after his retirement, and it was based on many years of performing and a varied career in magic. I feel he had much to say, and it was written in his own rather unique style. It depicts his time and his place in magic.

His true love of magic is the message that, in my opinion, connects the past with the present, upon which the future is built. I don't want it followed by anything else.

Gene's notebooks contain funny bits and pieces he jotted down over the years. Some he wrote, some he heard, some came from TV or radio. He didn't create them all.

> While Gene was still at home before he entered a
> nursing home his last few years, he said you might want
> the notebooks. So I asked you and sent them along. As I
> told you on the phone, *they are yours.* If you publish a
> book of them, it is *your* book. If you care to mention that
> Gene collected them, he might have liked that.

So there I was—with Gene Gordon's notebooks,
collected over all those years, with hundreds of
wonderful, laugh-filled lines that came from who
knows where, lines that Gene himself and I
personally thought funny. Some mildly funny, some
that created just a smile, some that struck me as
clever, others that were absolutely hilarious. All in
all, a wealth of good comedy material.

What I had, it finally sunk into my consciousness,
was a diary of patter Gene had kept over the years.
If properly organized and edited, this material could
become the nucleus of a book to share funny talk
with other magicians, comedians, and speakers.

Falling into Place

Sarah Mitchell, a young lady who started
packing mail orders for me when she was twelve,
now 21 and a junior in college, started entering
Gene's notebooks into the Macintosh computer in
January 1995 while on a school break. She finished
the job in May when school got out. That's how the
book got going.

My next step was to divide the jokes and lines into categories. Between school shows for two weeks in
May, I read and marked each line with a code.

I did some light editing along the way, including
the deletion of jokes I didn't like or which were out of

A sample from Gene's comedy notebooks, from which Sarah transcribed thousands of lines, jokes, and gags.

date. My basic criteria was this: If I didn't think the line was at least mildly amusing, I threw it out.

Then I created the chapter order and started entering the lines into the appropriate chapters. When my show schedule got too busy, Sarah finished entering the lines.

Some chapters seemed too short. I wrote new lines, remembered old things humorous, asked friends for lines to complete some parts and make them right. I delved into my college scrapbooks for more material. I finally put down on paper the "chicken crosses the road" chapter which I had lived for the last five years.

Friends Jan and Steve Taylor, Jeff Dickerson, Sarah and Bruce Johnson, Sammy Smith, Duane Laflin, Brenda and Marty Hahne, Virginia and Dick Williams, Roy Porfido, Sandy and John Gutherie, and Mark Merchant all helped out with comedy material and advice—and I thank them all. Finally, two wonderful teachers, Ruth Gordon and my high school English teacher, Gemma Roberts, read the

manuscript for grammar, punctuation, and anything else they didn't like. Their suggestions and
corrections were invaluable, and they ended up
making me look good!

All this combined to make me feel— inspired.

I also felt quite blessed. Ruth Gordon had blessed
me with the gift of the notebooks. Gene blessed me by
writing them and passing them on to me. Sarah
blessed me with coming home from college early and
being my other set of arms and legs for the month of
May. Without Sarah, *Laughter Legacy* would not
exist at this point in my busy life. So THANK YOU,
Ruth, Gene, and Sarah.

Who Are the People in Those Photos?

For the most part, the strange people you see in
these pages are members of my family, generations
back. While preparing this book, I visited my parents
and looked at the family scrapbooks. I loved the old
photographs and wanted to know who was who.
Some surprised me.

At that time, a thought had been running around
inside my head about my book, as well as all joke and
patter books I had ever read. The question was this:

*Who wants to read over 150 pages of line after
line, no matter how funny the lines are?*

I know I don't! After a dozen pages of straight
text, especially one-liners, things just start running
together.

My journalism training and experience said,
"You need to break up the text." I could see three
choices: with type variations, with line drawings, or
(you guessed it) with photos. As you will see, I used

all three, but most important were the old photographs to preserve the flavor of the book.

A book handed down from the past . . . to the present . . . for the future.

I hope you find the photos interesting, if not all laughable. But if you do laugh at some of them, don't feel bad. Hey, some are pretty funny! Since performing comedy often touches on real life, why not use *real people* to help illustrate the comedy?

My case is justified, at least to me.

In addition to the photos, let me add a hearty thanks once more to super magical illustrator Ed Harris for the fun cartoons he drew for the book. I love the way Ed takes my ideas and turns them into what I can only imagine, since I made just a C+ on the famous artists TV test.

Pictures make a book fun!

Your First Warning

"In dire seriousness, I have read an early portion of this manuscript. I shake my head in wonder over who, in his right mind, would purchase such a tome. In my day, the author of such verbage would be shot like a horse thief.

"My sincere advice is that you put this volume down and spend your hard-earned dollar on something more worth your while. Melville's classic Moby Dick *certainly comes to mind."*

—Sanford Pembrose Smith, editor, *The Dodge Tribune*

BABY QUIZ

For friends who knew Gene Gordon, try answering this question: One of the pictures on these two facing pages is of Gene Gordon as a baby. Which picture is Gene? And who is the person in the other photo? You'll find the answer on page 114.

He's Still Here

An amazing thing happened with a movie a few years back. The movie was all about one character, who was in the motion picture only for the last five minutes.

In the second *Star Trek* movie, Mr. Spock died, leaving loyal Trekkie fans in limbo for several years. The third film, *Star Trek III: The Search for Spock,* unfolded the story of Captain James Kirk's quest for a possible way of bringing his best friend, Spock, back to life. Sure, it was science fiction, but it sounded especially good to the fans!

My point is this: They spent the entire two-hour movie trying to get Spock back. He was not on screen until the last five minutes when we were elated to see his return. Yet, he was there—you could *feel his*

Don't you just love these old time oval-shaped photos? They're so—so . . . oh, what's the word?—QUAINT. So, folks, now that you've studied the two of them, which one is the real Gene Gordon? And who IS that other baby?

spirit—during the entire two hours. I considered it a miracle from that point of view.

Laughter Legacy has its similarity.

I can feel Gene Gordon in nearly every page of this book. He was born in 1903, so the old photographs, the times, and the clothing, would have been familiar to him. I'm sure he would have had some laughs at the pictures, as well as a handful of quips about them.

When I read the lines, I can hear his voice saying them. I can even read some of the lines that I have concocted and hear Gene saying them!

Now don't expect Gene to show up in person anytime soon. Elvis hasn't made his comeback, either! But Gene is here, his spirit saying, "Get out there and make those folks laugh, big folks or little ones, entertain them!"

I believe it.

Play with Words

Gene Gordon loved playing with words. He enjoyed double meanings, picking on himself, localizing humor to make it more effective, and leading the listeners down a word path, only to pull the rug out from under them at the last moment, just for a laugh.

He enjoyed, and understood, making people laugh. He loved playfully teasing kids on stage, asking them impossible questions to see their reactions.

Reading these pages will help you learn how to play with words, if you don't know how already. If you do, these pages will encourage you to play more.

The English language is a wonderful language for word play. According to Richard Lederer in *The Miracle of Language,* we have over 615,000 words in English, not to mention Southern American, which I claim to speak. The next nearest languages are German with 185,000 words, Russian with 130,000, and French with 100,000.

So let's use our abundance of words to create laughs!

It's New If You've Never Heard It

That is a saying I realized to be true a long time ago, especially when dealing with children's audiences. Why, I often use jokes or quips I learned in elementary and high school to make children in my school and library shows laugh today. The old jokes still work because the new children have never heard them!

That fact is a part of what *Laughter Legacy* is all about. Gene passed this material on to me, I've added to it, and I'm passing it on to you.

I honestly think you'll find something useful in these pages, something you can use to entertain people. I don't think you can read an entire page without finding something funny . . . and I'm quite serious about that.

It's A J-O-K-E!

There are times when I have delivered jokes in this book and received a groan for my efforts. Some even got applause.

In his book *Get Thee to a Punnery,* humorist Richard Lederer points out that the object of a pun is to *make* the listener groan. Perhaps the entire object of *any* corny material is to produce groans. As I've often said, "If they groan, at least they're not sitting there like stones."

And think of this: if your listeners groan, at least they're thinking! Hit your audience with enough groaners, and you can turn groans into laughter. After all, *a groan is as good as a laugh to a deaf elephant.*

Furthermore, if your joke is met with a groan, or just doesn't go over, have a planned ad-lib ready for a comeback. Maybe the ad-lib will get a laugh. Johnny Carson was a master at this. If you ever see any old "Tonight Show" monologues, watch the way Johnny handles jokes that didn't quite work. What an education!

In lectures and some shows over the last few years, I've used this catch phrase as a running gag: "IT'S A J-O-K-E!" And it's not just the wording, said at the moment I hear a groan coming or the instant I sense the audience didn't get or didn't like the quip I just made. It's all in the way I say those words.

If you see my video tape *Magic They Love To See,* you'll hear me say this several times in the comedy segment near the end. In print, the best way I can describe it is that I stretch out the word **J-O-K-E** into three beats or counts, whereas **IT'S** and **A** are only one beat or count each. After doing this several times in a performance, the audience catches on and often says "IT'S A J-O-K-E" along with me. That really adds to the fun for all.

Your Second Warning

"Somehow, we two did suspect that you ignored Mr. Sanford's cautionary words of wisdom. Now, this page presents your second chance at dashing these dull, most pitiful pages against the wall of the nearest red brick building. Take care to insure that a suitable trash receptacle rests just below the spot for which you aim, and do not miss. Whatever you do, dare not speak these utterances aloud before anyone for whom you attest affection."

—Stayworth F. Taylor, mayor of Rex, Georgia in 1897,
with his daughter Jelmine Caitbeth Taylor

Working Clean Funny

Some of the lines you'll read here are clever. Some are corny. Every one is clean. You will find no risque, blue, or dirty humor in these pages. Paraphrasing something Edgar Bergen once said, "If you're funny enough, you don't have to be dirty."

Dirty funny is easy: just throw a four-letter profanity or sexual innuendo into a joke, and you get a laugh based on shock value.

Clean funny is harder because you have to really THINK: *how can I make it funny without resorting to blue humor?* With the way sex and violence appear in everything these days, that's not easy. So much is acceptable today that wasn't 50, 30, 20, or even ten years ago. But that doesn't make it right. Just because TV and radio have anesthetized us into thinking it's okay to say certain four-letter words, that doesn't mean we all condone them. I don't. And you won't find any of those words here.

Gene Gordon could be funny without such jokes. David Ginn can be funny without them. So can you.

About five years ago, Laurel and Sammy Smith sat in Atlanta's Fox Theatre with Lynne and me having the time of our lives. For two hours and twenty minutes non-stop, we laughed and laughed, until tears rolled down our faces from the joy of a good time. We were watching Red Skelton in concert, telling his stories, doing his impersonations and characters, sharing his joy for comedy. He was 76 years old at the time.

At one point near the end of the show, Red said to the audience: "Isn't it wonderful that we can all be here laughing together without resorting to the use of profanity or four-letter language?" The audience unanimously roared its approval with applause. Red Skelton worked clean, and we loved him for that. *He didn't have to be dirty to be funny.*

Who Owns a Joke?

A long time ago in college, where I spent many an hour cooking up gag lines for cartoonists, I learned an important two-part truth:

Part One—you cannot copyright jokes. That's right. Ask the Library of Congress. Jokes are too short for copyright. And trademarks are a little on the expensive side!

Part Two—people in different places can think up the same joke or gag line. It honestly can happen and really DOES happen.

Once I saw a published cartoon that I thought was drawn by a cartoonist I wrote for. He had "held" a gag of mine with the same caption. When I didn't get paid for it, I wrote him, only to learn that the cartoon I saw (with my gag line) was done by another cartoonist who had my friend's same last name. Like minds think like thoughts!

In April 1987, I was working the Magic Castle in Hollywood. A fellow performer visited me between shows because he had heard we were both doing one of the same opening jokes. Obviously, that looked bad to people seeing both of us perform the same night in different rooms.

I instantly agreed to drop the joke from my act and let him continue with it. He asked where I'd heard the line because he thought it was original with him. In fact, he'd been doing it for twenty years.

Honestly, I couldn't remember where I had heard it. I don't think I ever heard *him* do it. A year later I was watching some old video clips I had dubbed off various TV shows in 1982-83. And there was comedian Gallagher on TNN's "Nashville Now" show doing the same gag!

My point is simple: if you don't want anyone to ever repeat or re-use your jokes, DON'T TELL THEM! If they're funny, Joe will share them with Bill at the office, Bill will repeat them to Frank, Frank will tell Helen at home, she'll tell her sister on the phone, who'll tell someone at church, who overhears a good line and uses it in a sermon or seminar, then it gets on radio or TV, where maybe Joe heard it in the first place.

And if I hear it anywhere in that chain, and it happens to fit the theme of my school or library show, I may tell it to the kids. To them, it is new and clever.

To my way of thinking, this is NOT STEALING. It is *sharing* humor and fun.

It would be an entirely different story if I sat in Mark Merchant's audience taking notes without permission, then started using his original material in my show across the street the next night. *That would be stealing.*

It would be a different matter if I taped the latest David Copperfield TV special, learned one of his routines almost ver batim, then performed it to make my living. *That would be stealing.*

It would be again a different matter if I listened to your comedy tape or video and wrote it into my book without permission. *That would be stealing.*

The material in this book is not stolen. It comes to you *shared* through Gene Gordon and David Ginn and a grapevine of people we will all never know, thanks to Joe and Bill and Frank and Helen and a thousand others.

Honestly, if there were any possible way—and there's not—to personally thank every person who thought up the lines in this book, I would. The best thing I can offer is a big bold-face **THANK YOU** and the knowledge that YOU had something to do with making the world a happier place in which to live and laugh. Indeed, YOU are a part of this *Laughter Legacy.*

Writing and Speaking

Somewhere along the line, Gene picked up this quote, which I have excerpted from his notebooks:

"Writing, after all, is nothing but speaking on paper. Speaking is nothing but thinking out loud. And thinking is nothing but silent speech. A man should write the way he talks."

That struck me as interesting. Why? Because the best writing advice I ever got in journalism school was during an English class. The professor said: "Write the way you talk."

Assuming you can speak well, you can also write well. I have gone about my writing in that way. Some people didn't understand this until they heard me speak for the first time at a lecture. When they heard my Southern American accent, these people told me that I write just the way I sound. Readers also tell me that later they can read my books and actually *hear me* saying the words to them!

Beware! After seeing David Ginn at a lecture, workshop, or convention—even hearing me on an audio or a video tape—you might become Southern Americanized! This would automatically cause you to say CO-COLA instead of Coca-Cola!

I write as I speak because I want to be me. I am the only one who can be me, just as you are the only one who can be you.

When you read *Laughter Legacy,* you'll read things as David Ginn or Gene Gordon or one of our friends might say them. We've thought them, said them, written them down for *you.* The lines are there for you, but the exact words may not *be* you.

Your job is to *make them you.* Figure out how you will say them. Practice them, both in your head and out loud. Try them on audiences, a few friends here and there, then bigger audiences. Trial and error. Make mistakes. Have the adventure of discovering what is *you* and how *you* can be funny.

The material is here for you. It's funny if you've never heard it. And even if they have heard it, that same line could be funny again just in the way *you* deliver it.

DAVID GINN
4387 St. Michaels Drive
Lilburn, GA 30047 USA

MAY 1995 - October 1997

A Special Note: My single regret about this book is that my dad, Frank Ginn, did not live to see its publication. He read my rough draft, offered suggestions, even laughed at that cover photo in his hospital bed his last day on earth. He left us on May 10, 1997, shortly after midnight. Lynne assures me, however, that God will arrange for Daddy to see the finished product. Heaven has its ways. Meanwhile, Dad, we're alive and hanging in here on planet earth, praise the Lord! And we miss you.

Your Third Warning

Obviously, if you have perused this volume thus far, you are one of those "gluttons for punishment," which you shall have before these pages conclude. My dear wife Jilliana and eldest daughter Denustasia were blinded by reading some of these words. Fortunately, little Aurelia and Childsforth cannot read, so they were spared this misfortune. Take heed! Destroy this book! Buy more copies to destroy! Save the world from this insidiusness.

—Davis Wade, Gwinnett Postal Inspector

1. Introductions

GENE GORDON felt that a good MC should get the acts on with the use of clever dialogue. The words which follow reflect that concept, some subtly humorous, some boldly funny.

Besides introducing people, a performer can use some of these words to introduce other things—acts, effects, tricks, songs, poetry, whatever.

The real point is to put your audience at ease and help them welcome what comes next. Your words can do that.

• Good ladies, evening and gentlemen. That does it! Next time I'll rehearse everything!

• I am not here to sell you oil stock, chewing gum, or long distance telephone service.

• This boy has an act that's out of this world—and I can't think of a better place for it.

• Next week I'll be here in person.

• The next number is a mystifying little problem from India, the Land of Magic. The Hindu conjurors have a world-wide reputation for the seemingly impossible things they can do. Among them is the

Indian Rope Trick, which has mystified thousands of
tourists, who annually visit India, the wonderland of
the universe.

• I'm glad to be . . . what's the word? . . . HERE.

• This show starts at eight o'clock sharp and
ends at ten o'clock dull.

• I am the MC. That means Monotony Creator.
Or is it Monkey Coordinator?

• My job, as I understand it, is to entertain you.
Your job, as I understand it, is to watch and listen.
If you finish your job before I do mine, just hold up
your hands.

• I'll never forget what my speech teacher told
me. She said, "In promulgating your esoteric
cogitations and articulating your superficial
sentimentalities, always beware of platitudinous
ponderosity." Then she advised me to "forget all
affectations of rodomontade profundity." I looked all
that up. It means: *"Don't use big words!"*

• They told me to say something warm and
gracious, so I will. Gracious, isn't it warm in here
tonight?

• I'm the Mastoid of Ceremonies. Of course, a
mastoid is a pain in the ear. *(Steve Taylor)*

• I take pride in the fact that I have given this
next young man a lot of advice which he completely
ignored and went on to success.

The well-dressed Master of Ceremonies, around 1941: my father, James Franklin Ginn.

• May I quote to you from Lewis Carroll's famous classic book, *Alice's Adventures in Wonderland,* or, as it is more commonly known, *Alice in Wonderland.* In the middle of Chapter Five, we have this dialogue between Alice and the Queen of Hearts:

> "I can't believe that," said Alice.
> "Can't you?" said the Queen, in a pitying tone. "Try again. Draw a deep breath and shut your eyes."
> Alice laughed. "There's no use trying," she said. "One can't believe in impossible things."
> "I daresay you haven't had much practice," said the Queen. "When I was your age, I always did it for half an hour a day. Why, sometimes I've believed as many as six impossible things before breakfast."

Well, the Queen was right. And during this show I am going to ask you to practice believing impossible things for the next few minutes. I have more than six things to show you, and I assure you, they are all quite impossible . . . but you can believe them if you try.

• I was surprised when your secretary called me up and invited me here. I was surprised because I don't have a telephone.

• *Double act intro.* These next two performers need no introduction. It so happens they know each other.

• A little applause frightens our next performer, so let's give him a big hand and scare the dickens out of him!

• Shakespeare said: "If I am deceived, I hope I may know it. But if I know it, I hope I may be able to laugh at the whole affair." So if I play tricks on you during this performance, just laugh it off!

• Perhaps some of you are wondering why I sent for you. It's very simple. I wanted—*(pause a moment)*—an audience.

• It has been said that *Performer's Name* is the greatest magician the world has ever known. And now, meet the man who said it—*Same Performer's Name.*

• His act looks like a million . . . like a million other acts.

• If there is anything about this convention—the shows, the food, the rooms, the displays—that you don't like, the committee wants you to please keep it to yourself because they are tired of hearing it.

• I have performed on the same stage with many magicians, and I want to say this about our next artist—he was one of them.

ON THE AIR

LADIES AND GENTLEMEN, WE LIVE IN A WORLD THAT DOESN'T MAKE SENSE—AND THIS SHOW IS A SYMBOL OF OUR TIMES.

2. Applause

MOST TIMES, people applaud when they are happy. And, typically, people are happy when they are applauding. The more they applaud, the happier they are, because they are applauding, because they are happy. As an entertainer, my job—*your job*—is to do things and say things to make the audience applaud and to make them happy. That applause makes us performers happy, too.

There are many ways we can do this. Magicians and jugglers can do astounding feats. Clowns, comedians, ventriloquists can say or do funny things. If you make the audience members laugh enough, they end up applauding you. Why? Because you made them feel good. You made them happy.

These days people are so accustomed to watching TV, performers often have to "tell" the audience, "It's okay to applaud. It's okay to express yourselves, as an audience, in that way." This is especially true with children, who have not yet been conditioned to being a proper audience.

Sometimes a joking remark is all it takes to kick an audience from smiles, laughter and amazement into applause. That's what this chapter is all about. Pick your favorites.

• Thank you for that spontaneous burst of heavy breathing.

• Please, folks, put down those remotes. This is *not* TV! It's a live show. You can really clap your hands and applaud if you want to!

• Thank you for the applause—I deserve it.

• Please—no applause. Virtue is its own reward.

• *One person claps.* Don't think it's easy getting applause like that. I had to pay him good money.

• Please don't applaud. You'll wake up the others.

• Your applause was deafening. I couldn't hear a thing.

• *Weak applause:* I guess you're not sure.

• Thank you very much—that's too much.

• Some monks in a religious order have taken a vow of silence which forbids even the clapping of hands. I think a lot of them are here tonight.

• That's what I like—a clap happy audience.

• You should have seen last night's show. I had them in the aisles—trying to get out!

• Before I do this dangerous feat, which might possibly fail and cause mortal injury to my victim—*I mean volunteer*—perhaps you could share with me the applause you might give if indeed it does work. That's all? Start praying, George!

• Thanks for the applause. May I congratulate you on your intelligence.

• Don't applaud. I'm just at the age where I get frightened so easily.

• Some magicians say that applause makes them nervous, but it never bothers me.

• Now, I'd like to say a word regarding applause during this performance. Some people are not in the habit of applauding, but it's a good habit to form. Recently, a doctor told me that clapping your hands stirs up the circulation. In fact, he estimated that a few minutes of good brisk applause is so beneficial that it extends anyone's life by several months. So this evening, let's all insure ourselves of living to a ripe old age, shall we?

• I know why you don't applaud. It's quite obvious. You're overcome with astonishment.

• Ladies and gentlemen, let's all give a good round of applause to the *handkerchiefs!*

• *Good applause:* Sounds like my relatives finally got here.

• I got more applause than that at the Lake Shore Funeral Parlor.

One of Gene Gordon's audiences, circa 1930 in Kentucky. Notice that the dog appears to be more "into the show" than the humans. At least they dressed for the performance. This picture shows the group before Gene used some of these lines to "warm them up." Or was it during?

• Was that applause or just someone spanking a baby?

• Thank you for the applause. I'll remember you to my dying moments—and I usually have a few about this time each day.

• Don't applaud. Just stand out in the aisles and kneel in homage.

• I've been watching you. Some of you didn't applaud.

• Believe me, you won't hurt my concentration by applauding.

• Thank you, I'll take a bow. I'll take another—it's good for my figure.

• That's a nice smile you have. Could you make it a little louder?

• This place is cold, but if you keep applauding, we can all keep warm.

Reading these applause lines and gags reminds me of the Robert Orben material I read, studied, memorized, practiced, and used as a teenager. One of my favorites read: "Please don't applaud, just throw money."

One night, as a 16-year-old magician, I said that line at a scout camp performance. Moments later a half dozen pennies arrived at my feet—and a quarter hit me in the forehead. I never used that line again!

3. Audience Remarks

YOU'LL FIND two categories here: (1) Remarks you make to certain audience members, and (2) Remarks you offer to the entire audience. I have purposely not separated them. Study them as a whole, and decide which is which yourself.

As you study them, get a feel for how to joke with your audience, how to blend together with them through humor.

Listen to other comedians to sense how they let their audiences know they are joking, kidding around, making fun—though sometimes the performer doesn't say that.

How can you, during your own delivery, cause your listeners to understand that? That you are playing with them, using words, for the fun of it? That is one of your goals.

• I like that coat. What time do you feed it?

• I know you all have problems, but don't think of them now!

• I can't wait for you—hurry up when you laugh.

• These jokes are like pitching. I just throw them. You have to catch them.

• Oh, yes, there's great excitement at the rear and murmurs of "Marvelous! I don't understand how he does it!"

• If you can't laugh at the jokes of the age, then laugh at the age of the jokes.

• I just tell my jokes—I don't explain them. In fact, I won't tell you any new ones tonight. I'll just refresh your memory.

• No shouting or cheering please. Just ordinary applause.

• If I have said anything to offend you, I can repeat it.

• For the next few moments, I'm going to entertain and amaze myself with several fantastic effects—I hope you folks will feel free to join me at anytime.

• When you laugh, it proves you are still barbarians at heart—you love to see someone else suffer!

• You have probably noticed that I am a man of many words and little ability.

• Stop! The first laugh is all I want.

• That was just a throw-away gag. I should have thrown it away long ago.

• If I make any suspicious moves, please call my attention to it.

• You make silence such a wonderful thing to look forward to.

• I can see that you're going to be a wonderful audience. In fact, I feel like one of you already. I don't know which one of you I feel like, but whoever he is—he'd better go home and lie down.

• Everytime I look out over an audience, the question comes to my mind: Is there anyone out there who could do these tricks better than I can? That's the question I ask myself. I might add that I never wait for an answer.

• Go ahead—leave. The believers will stay here.

• I know that wasn't very good, but it didn't take very long.

• Now don't laugh too much. I'm a firm advocate of mirth control.

• Hurry up and sit down—nobody will notice you are late.

• Sit down and see the rest of the show for nothing.

• I can write shorthand, but it takes me longer.

• *No laugh:* Well, maybe you're right.

• Some day you're going to laugh like that in a zoo and find yourself engaged to a hyena.

• It's nothing—and nearly all of you realized it.

• I'm getting bored with this, so I can imagine how you feel.

• *To talkative person:* I'm sorry, but we're not having audience participation tonight.

• When I ask people what the most boring thing is, they never seem to know. So I'll tell you. It's taking a ride on a certain train in Australia for 328 miles without one curve or crossing a river. During the entire ride, you will not see one single tree.

When I ask them what the second most boring thing is, they say, "Wait until you finish your show. Then we'll tell you."

I wonder where Gene found this statistic? I understand from some down under friends that it refers to the Nullarbor Plain, and it is true. Gene mentions it in his classic "Favorite Comedy Mind-Reading Act" from the **Magical Legacy** *book. When I personally have performed that routine, I always tack on the lines: "If you take that train ride, be sure to carry a long book to read. It's a very boring trip." No, we can't call it a real knee-slapper, but mildly it amuses, the sort of thing Gene enjoyed a lot.*

• That's one of my Easter jokes. It always lays an egg.

• *To late-comers:* I'm glad you finally got here. We had you marked absent.

• Remember, when you smile you add to your face value.

• I see a man sleeping out there. I really don't mind his sleeping, but at least he could have said, "Goodnight."

• I don't blame the baby for crying. He probably just found out where he is.

• Sure, go ahead and laugh. Tomorrow you'll hate yourself for it.

• I know you believe you understand what you think I said, but I am not sure you realize that what you heard is not what I meant.

• How can this be a battle of wills—and I'm losing?

• When I *try* to tell a joke, I wish you would *try* to laugh.

• Will everyone please take a deep breath and blow toward the stage. Ah, I love the air conditioning they have in here! It's man-made!

• I really don't mind people looking at their watches. It's when they start shaking them that gets me mad.

• Have you enjoyed yourselves? When you get home, you can send me a C.A.R.E. package.

• I have the feeling I'm being stared at.

• In a short time I had the audience in the palm of my hand. That gives you an idea of the size of the audience.

• I didn't come here to be made sport of. *(No? Where do you usually go? —Jeff Dickerson)*

• *To a baby in the audience.* There's no use in you crying. I don't have the time to listen to your problems now.

• Let me announce at this time that I have discontinued long talks on account of my throat. Several people have threatened to cut it.

• You ARE allowed to laugh aloud in here, you know.

• There seems to be a little undercurrent of sacrilegious snickering going on down in the audience. Pay attention now, as I may ask questions later.

• Services for that joke will be held at ten o'clock tomorrow morning.

4. Animals

BILL LARSEN SR., years ago in *Genii Magazine,* described his idea of the perfect kids' birthday show. It went something like this:

For a 30-minute party, start by producing a dove. Let the kids take turns holding the dove for about 15 minutes, then put the dove away.

Then produce a live rabbit. Let the kids pet the rabbit for 15 minutes. That ends the show. Collect your check and leave!

My paraphrase of Bill's concept points out how much kids love animals. In fact, we're all "suckers" for a cute little furry creature, such as a live bunny.

Giving animals personalities in your performance makes them more "human" to your audience. Always name your animals, and be sure you tell the children the animals' names.

For example, in years past I really enjoyed performing a trick called "Farmyard Frolics." In that routine I had pictures of five animals: a cow named Daisy (see Chapter 9 for what I said about her), a pig named Porky ("He hates barbeque!"), a sheep named Laddy the Lamb ("He grows wool coats and we cut them off to make jackets!"), a cat named Jet ("He can

1925. Frank Ginn, nicknamed "Pete" at the time (which he hated), rides a very unusual five-legged mule at the old home place in Lithonia, Georgia.

In those days it was not peculiar to see deformed animals on a farm, due to the lack of medical techniques which we know today.

disappear at will—anybody here named Will?"), and a Dog named Rover.

Rover is the smartest dog in the world. At least that's what my friends down on the farm told me. Well, I didn't believe it. So they told me to ask Rover a few questions.

I said, *"Rover, what's on that tree over there?"* And the dog said, "BARK! BARK!"

Then I said, *"Rover, what's on top of the house?"* And the dog said, "ROOF! ROOF!"

Next I asked him, *"Rover, what is the texture of sandpaper?"* And the dog said, "RUFF! RUFF!"

"Wait a minute," I told my friends. "This is getting just a little bit deep, as in hard to believe." But they persisted. They told me the dog watched lots of old TV shows. "Ask him a question about that," they insisted.

So I asked the dog, *"Rover, what was Jackie Gleason's character name on the Honeymooners?"* And the dog said, "RALPH! RALPH!"

I shook my head. "This is ridiculous!" I exclaimed to my rural friends. "You're just trying to fool a city boy!"

"No, no," they insisted. "Rover really is smart. Ask him just one more question—ask him something about sports. He loves sports."

"All right," I said, "but this is the very last question." I looked that dog straight in the eye and asked, *"Rover, who was the greatest baseball player of all time?"*
And the dog said, "RUTH! RUTH!"
Immediately I shouted, "UH—UH—UH!"
So the dog said, *"HANK AARON?"*
Folks, that was one smart dog!

So here are some words about animals to help you create more personality in that part of your act.

• I'll make a rabbit appear on your head. One, two, three—grab it! Do you feel the hare?

• I trained my dog to eat only when I ring a bell. Guess what happened? Last week he ate up the Avon lady!

• Worms used to come in pairs, but now they come in apples.

• I know of an old elephant who had a toothache in his tusk. They had to pull it, but they couldn't get the tusk out. So he went to Alabama because there the *tusk-a-loosa.*

• In Australia, there isn't a single fly. They're all married and have large families.

• A little chick saw an orange in his nest and chirped out, "Oh, look at the orange marmalade!" *(Momma laid.)*

• I had a case of puppy love, and I've never liked dogs since.

• A man was sitting by a fire in his house on a cold, snowy night. Suddenly he heard a knock at the door. *(Knock on something.)* He went to the door and opened it, but saw no one. Then he noticed a lowly snail on the doorstep.

"Please, sir, I'm freezing out here in the snow. Could I come inside for a moment and warm myself by your fire?"

Without a word, the gruff man kicked the snail far out into the snow, slammed the door, and went back to his fire.

Two years later. *(Knock again.)* The same man got up from his fire, went to the door, and opened it. It was the same snail.

The snail said, "Excuse me—was that a NO?"

• A bee stung me once, and I went to the beekeeper and complained. I said I expected him to do something about it. He said he certainly would—if I would just show him which bee it was, he would punish it.

• Peanuts must be fattening. After all, have you ever seen a thin elephant?

• Two silkworms had a race, but they ended up in a tie.

• Do you see that dog? *(Invisible)* If you do, you're in trouble.

• *About your rabbit:* He keeps dreaming he's a chicken and cackling during the night. I don't mind the cackling, but what am I going to do with all those eggs?

• I hear a crow lives for two hundred years. I'm going to keep this one and see if it's true.

• My dog is smart. He can read. If a sign says "Keep off the Grass," he will. Or if a sign says "Wet Paint," he will.

• A missionary met a lion in the jungle. The missionsary fell to his knees, praying. So did the lion. The missionary was pleased and told the lion as much. The lion said, "Don't interrupt. I'm saying grace."

Circa 1920. The modern extended family goes fishing in beautiful St. Petersburg, Florida. The sum at day's end: just a few fish, but large ones. Pictured in real life are (back row, left to right): Aunt Fleta (Gussie's sister), Uncle Jim Cheshire (in hat), Ivey Barksdale and his wife, Lucy Barksdale (Gussie's baby sister). Front row: Aunt Lula (Gussie's oldest sister) and, finally, Gussie Smith, my wife Lynne's grandmother.

• This collar is guaranteed to keep anyone free from fleas for ninety days.

• Bears are funny. They are born with a fur coat, then they sleep all through the *only* season where they need a fur coat. During other seasons, a fur coat is—pardon the expression—*unbearable*.

• My best punch was a rabbit punch—but they never let me fight rabbits.

• My friend had a dog who played classical piano. At a concert, somebody coughed. The dog jumped off his stool and chased the man right out of the auditorium. But the man had nothing to worry about. The dog's Bach was worse than his bite.

• When I tell people that my rabbit is just like one of the family, they always ask which one.

Before carpool, you could "mule-pool!" Here is Len, Emmett, and Fred Ginn, my grandfather, @ 1903 on the farm in Lithonia, Georgia.

• It's nice for children to have pets until the pets start having children.

• My dog's name is Ginger. She doesn't bite, but once in a while Ginger snaps.

5. Education

READING THIS? You must have some education already! If you bought this book to read, you're really smart! If you use some of this to lift up laughter to your audiences, you truly have my respect.

We'll play with schooling, now—elementary, high school or higher education on the university level. I'll even play with college life even more in a later chapter, on a more personal level.

Even though you'll be reading school joking lines here, let me emphasize that I am totally for learning in school and all of life. As my friend Harold Taylor admonished me in his seventies, "Never stop learning." I believe that. But I can still joke, can't I?

• All my life I've been devoted to the three R's— Relaxing, Reclining and Resting.

• I'm taking a new non-credit college course. It's called "How to Get Someone Else to Do It."

• My fourth grade teacher didn't teach history— she remembered it!

The typical school class picture of 1929. Here is Miss Tatum's 3rd Grade at Gordon Elementary School, in East Atlanta, Georgia. Back row, 2nd from right is Helen Matthews, my mother; and second row, 5th from left, is Frank Ginn, my father. Married in 1941, they've know each other over 75 years!

• I was musically inclined when I was a child. I played on the floor. When I was older I went to a musical college—Sing Sing!

• A quick study? Why, I took a four-year course in Ignorance and made it in three years.

• I got a scholarship to a medical college, but they didn't want me while I was alive.

• A college education never hurt anyone as long as he is willing to learn something afterward.

• All he wants out of school is himself.

• When I was a kid, I was so thin the teacher kept marking me absent.

• Fourth grade? I was in the fourth grade so long, the other kids thought I was the teacher! *(Steve or Jan Taylor)*

• I couldn't help it if I didn't do well in school. My teacher was always saying, "Look, Stupid!" and I did.

• A pronoun? That's a noun that gets paid.

• I learned this at Magic School under the G.I. Bill. That may not mean much to you, but I think it's pretty good considering the fact that I was never in the military at all.

• Hospital for sick birds: Poly Clinic.

• Kids today have all the answers, except at examination time.

• I played hookey from correspondence school. Sent them empty envelopes.

• In school I was as smart as the next fellow. Was it my fault they always put me next to an idiot?

• What grade are you in? Third? My third grade teacher always respected me. She had to—I was older than she was.

• How is your deportment in school? Is your teacher in favor of having you deported?

• The modern child's idea of roughing it is to have to do his homework with the TV set turned off.

• I was an early astronaut. Even in high school I took up space.

• I only went to school one day. That was to find out when vacation began.

• It seems a shame that a college education should be wasted on high school graduates, who already know everything.

• Even a professor discovers how little he knows when a child begins to ask questions.

• Know what you call the road to the psychology department? The psycho-path. *(Steve Taylor)*

• You learn diction by filling your mouth with marbles. Every day you try to talk clearly right through the marbles, and every day you lose one marble from your mouth. When you've lost all your marbles, you are then a perfect speaker.

• Boy, I'll never forget my school days. I was the teacher's pet. She kept me in a cage. For the first week of school, I thought I was a gerbil!

• When he won his letter in college, somebody had to read it to him.

• I was graduated MAGIC CUM LOUDER.

• I asked him what the first thing was he learned in school. He said he learned to pollute the flag.

Atlantans 'Wowed' By GI's Appetite

ATLANTA, July 9—(AP)—Diners at an Atlanta cafeteria lost interest in their own food when Pfc. Chester J. Salvatori, the Army's eating wonder, placed his order.

They stared goggle-eyed when the Southbridge, Mass., soldier, a mere 121-pounder, put away:

Seven orders of fried chicken, 10 orders of French fried potatoes, nine glasses of orange juice, two quarts of milk, 10 combination salads, five egg salads, two orders of olives, two glasses of iced coffee, two slices of watermelon, five orders of rolls and five slices of apple pie a la mode.

Salvatori, who had his first pass in more than four weeks yesterday, was eating light. He said six candy bars and a quart of ice cream before dinner had taken the edge off his appetite.

Salvatori's voracious eating habit was attributed by Col. Burgh S. Burnet, post surgeon at Fort McPherson, to exhibitionism. He said the soldier enjoyed the Ohs and Ahs of onlookers to such an extent that he had eventually developed the habit of eating vast quantities.

A French horn player with a special service band, Salvatori was admitted to the fort hospital about a month ago for observation. As a cure, the hospital removed his audience and is gradually cutting down on his food.

6. Food

MOM SAID: "Don't play with your food." But she never said, "Don't make fun of it," or did she? Whichever advice you choose to follow, we'll spend these next few pages joking about what you have or had to eat. Now let's get on to the meat of the chapter. Wishing you happy digestion.

• Over-eating makes you thick to your stomach.

• I don't drink coffee. I'll just have cream and sugar.

• The best way to serve spinach is to somebody else.

• Sure I know what a pickle is. A pickle is a cucumber soured by a jarring experience.

• It was a honeymoon salad—just lettuce alone.

• What did the grape say when the elephant stepped on it? It didn't say anything—it just let out a little wine.

• Two books influenced my early life the most: my mother's cookbook and my father's checkbook.

• Two peanuts were walking through a dark alley. One was mugged and the other was assaulted.

• It's time to go. Or, as they said at the salad bar, "Lettuce leaf!"

• Definition of a vegetarian: A salad citizen. *(Jan Taylor)*

• What did the Baby Corn say to the Momma Corn? "Where's Pop Corn?" Ooooh—that's corny!

• Everywhere you look these days you read about organically-grown foods. I want to know—are other foods IN-ORGANICALLY GROWN?

David Ginn himself, age 16 months. This is one of my early magic tricks. It's called the "Vanishing Pear" trick. Just close your eyes. Now the pear is gone from my fork!

• Supermarket? That's a place where you spend 30 minutes looking for instant coffee.

• I was thinking of you at lunch today. I was eating alphabet soup, and your name came up.

• I have a new way to reduce. I eat everything I want. I just don't swallow!

• *George Overton, my friend Susan Blanken-ship's grandfather, used to word it a different way. He said the perfect diet was this:* **If it tastes good, spit it out!**

• At lunch he swallowed a spoon and now he can hardly stir.

• He eats so fast that he makes sparks come out of his knife and fork.

• Flies come into this restaurant to commit suicide.

• Where were the world's first donuts made? In Greece.

• I wonder if I'll ever find a waiter with courage enough to lay the check face up?

• I drink so much clam juice that my hair rises and falls with the tide.

• Chief Shortcake died. His wife refused to have an undertaker. She just kept repeating, "Squaw bury Shortcake."

• You put on weight when you exceed the feed limit.

• I ordered a steak and a few kind words. When my waitress brought the steak, I said, "Where are the few kind words?" She said, "Don't eat the steak!"

• A fellow in Australia rushed into a restaurant and shouted, "Help, Mates, I've just swallowed a boomerang!" Do you know they threw him out of that place ten times before they believed him?

• I only tried to speak French once. Trying to impress a waitress, I said to her, "A cup of coffee, *s'il vous plait.*" So she brought me a cup of coffee and a seafood plate.

7. Clothing

ROY PORFIDO and I were riding somewhere in Sacramento, California, with Roy driving. I pointed to a lady having car trouble:

"Look at that lady in distress," I said.

Roy pointed to a tanned blonde in a short white skirt and said, "I'd rather look at the lady in DAT DRESS!"

"Dis-dress. Dat-dress," I said. "That's good, Roy. I'll use it some way. And I'll give you credit."

So two years ago I did a movie routine using Abbott's Arrowhead in my "Wild West Magic Show." I told the girl as she sat on the stool, "You'll play the lady in distress. Of course, you're not wearing DIS-DRESS—you're wearing this pair of shorts!"

Corny, but clean, and it did get a mild laugh. What did you expect? A guffaw?

I've picked on clothing worn by children, teens, and adults before. So have a lot of others, including Uncle Gene. All you have to remember is this: *make it obvious that you are picking on their clothing PLAYFULLY, not insulting them.* "I just love your earrings," I might say to a girl wearing the kind that dangle. "They're long enough for Tarzan to swing on!"

• You can easily beat the high prices of meat and clothing. Become a vegetarian nudist.

A fashionable church audience in the early part of this century. Sitting front row, 3rd from left, is my grandmother, Ida Grey Ginn.

• What kind of clothing do lawyers wear? Why— law suits!

• I would have worn my tux, but my penguin is using it.

• Do you like my shoes? I get them at PayMore. *(Sandy Gutherie)*

• *About clown outfit:* Do you like my new suit? Its by Calvin Clown. *(Sandy Gutherie)*

January 18, 1896, is the actual date on the back of this photograph. Obviously, these folks were well-dressed with the intention of seeing a David Ginn or Gene Gordon magic show. The problem is: neither of us was born yet!

• The cheaper the stockings, the more of a run a girl gets for her money.

• *To boy wearing boots:* Are those real cowboy boots? Are you a real cowboy?

Now here are three from Duane Laflin:

• I once got so confused I put ketchup on my shoelaces and tied knots in my french fries.

• What did the necktie say to the hat? You go ahead while I just hang around.

• How do sailors get their clothes clean? They throw them overboard, and they wash ashore.

• I just bought a topless, bottomless, frontless, backless piece of clothing. How do you like my new belt?

• This new perfume comes all the way from Paris. It's called "Nothing." It's blend of aromas ensures that you will create a sensation going to a party wearing "Nothing."

• I hate to see a family in cheap clothing, unless it's mine.

• That's a nice hat. Your head holds it up so well.

• This is my new sport coat. How do you like the stripes? I drew them on here myself.

• Why, I had this suit custom-made in Hong Kong . . . using the finest virgin wool, herringbone buttons, silk thread, genuine rhinestones, and water buffalo leather support stitching. Took them all of 15 minutes to do it.

• My sister used to wear a scarf around her neck. I think it kept her head from falling off.

• Nothing lasts as long as clothes you don't like.

• I have a suit for every day of the year. How do you like it?

• I bought my first tuxedo when I got out of high school. How do you like it?

• He opened the door in his pajamas—funny place to keep a door. *(This reminds me of my favorite old Groucho Marx line: "Africa! Africa! This morning I woke up and shot an elephant in my pajamas! How he got in my pajamas, I'll never know!")*

8. Magic Tricks

MOST EVERYONE enjoys magic to some degree. Most people are intrigued by it. Using humor to explain (or sorta-pseudo-explain) your tricks is a good way to throw spectators off-guard and keep them guessing. A good joke or gagline can even be the key to misdirection in a trick.

Reading the word play that follows will explain itself.

• Count 30 cards. I'll help you when you get to 20.

• I have tricks too humorous to mention.

• I'll change this stick of gum into a piece of candy. One! Two! *Drop the gum to the floor.* Oops! Did you see the gum drop?

• Doing these tricks is just the same as doing anything else. It only looks different.

• This mystery comes from the far east—as far east as Boston. *(Name any town east of your show.)*

• My last effect is "The Exit" by special request.

• I know a magician who performs this trick, and he can't use this hand. I won't let him. It belongs to me.

• Keep your eyes open while I do this trick. You won't be able to see it if you don't.

• I used to do this when I was young and foolish. I'm not young anymore.

• I can do this with three decks—one at a time.

• Be patient—love will find a way.

• I drop them once in awhile to show they are not tied together.

• There are exactly 672 stitches in this hank. If you don't believe me, count them yourself.

• I nearly bought a handkerchief myself this afternoon, but they wanted $12.00 for it. I thought that was too much to blow in.

• I turn the scarf around to show the center is in the middle on both sides.

• When I play poker, I usually win. When I play the horses, I usually lose. I can't shuffle horses.

• I will say a few magic words in Hindu, something that you don't understand—and I don't either.

• Some call this sleight of hand, while others call it prestidigitation. I call it bread and butter.

• My hands are quite empty—they have never been in politics.

• This trick can be done in many forms—including chloroform.

• Like the magic tale of old, where it goes—no one knows.

• Fifty-eight generations have passed since Caesar paced the streets of Rome, but the Linking Rings were popular then. It is only six generations since Napoleon walked the streets of Toulon contemplating suicide—the Rings were popular then. As old as the hills, yet as popular today as they were thousands of years ago.

• While learning this trick, I went for six days without any sleep. I did my sleeping nights.

• I'd like to borrow a handkerchief—any size, any color, any nationality. I call it equal opportunity.

• This is an old Chinese experiment based on an ancient teaching that everything is, even if it isn't.

• Kindly stand on your head when you see your card.

• I do this for my own amazement.

• Shuffle the cards—I'll pick them up.

• Please notice that I do not swallow the card or push it under my fingernail.

• Memorize the cards so you will know I am not

trying to deceive you as that would be beneath my dignity as a magician.

• These cards travel, invisibly, singly, in couples, triplets, and quadruplets, and without the aid of a taxi.

• Will you kindly examine this envelope? Just step inside and have a walk around to be sure no one's there.

• The egg has vanished—where do you think it's gone? Up my sleeve? Oh, no, I may laugh up my sleeve, but I don't throw eggs up there.

David Ginn, age 3. "Before I was into magic, I was into winning trophies and wearing capes." I don't know where the cape is now, but the trophy sits proudly in the unfinished part of my basement.

• I'd like a gentleman's handkerchief. Is there one in the audience—a handkerchief, I mean?

• This next trick took me from complete obscurity to utter oblivion.

• The quickness of the hands deceives the feet.

• Some call this art by the name *hypnotism.* Others call it mesmerism. But I call it—rheumatism.

• Scientists have been endeavoring for years to find something like this. *(Hold up object.)* I am a scientist myself, having taken a three week course in the International Correspondence Schools, so I'll give you my version.

• That's a pretty good trick, is it not? Yes, it is— NOT!

• Believe it or not, Ripley saw me do this trick, and believe it or not, he still doesn't believe it!

• Magician holds a rubber hammer in his hand during a trick and says, "Do you want a local or general anesthetic?"

• I wish I was sitting out there with you folks. I'd like to see this trick myself!

• Before the trick climax using a helper: "Watch closely—your big moment in life is at hand!"

• I'll never forget this trick if I live to be normal.

• Is there anyone here who can say why I shouldn't restore this torn napkin? If so, speak now, or forever hold the pieces.

• *Transportation effect:* Now I will give you a demonstration of wireless transmission, by means of which an object may be moved from one place to another with such remarkable rapidity that it seems hard to imagine that the place in which it is found to be placed, after it was placed in the first place, is not the same place as the place in which it was in the first place placed.

• In magic, you need imagination. You know, *imagination*—what you put in deductions on your income tax.

• This trick is so old that the last time it was performed, history wasn't even a subject in school.

• If you want to figure that out, you'll have to use your own figures.

• A lot of these things can't be explained. You know, for business reasons.

• For performing this trick, I received from the University of Siberia two degrees—below zero.

• *Confetti on stage.* You probably won't remember my act, but the clean-up man will never forget me.

• This is safe. It works nine times out of ten. I have already performed it nine times.

• Day after day I stand here and wonder how I do it. My wife wonders why I do it. I can see by your faces that you wish I *wouldn't do it!*

• This is a first grade trick. The trouble is, people above the first grade never appreciate it.

• I'm doing this behind my back because I was a backwards child.

I DID THE TRICK RIGHT—THE CARDS JUST DIDN'T COOPERATE!

• You know, sometimes I think there must be a trick to this.

• Howard Thurston actually invented this trick. He thought nothing of it. I can see you folks think the same as Thurston.

• Some people think, in perfecting my tricks, that I must have spent years of hard labor. Others think I *deserve* years AT hard labor.

• I do my best tricks around two o'clock in the morning, so I hope you folks don't mind staying around for a while.

• I hate to do all this. It's so deceitful!

• I was planning to do a medley of Polynesian war chants and South Sea bird calls at this time, but instead I have substituted this trick.

• Some magic tricks can actually be traced back thousands of years to the early magic marvels of the Persians or the Chinese. This next marvel was invented last week in Decatur *(name small town nearby)*.

• Keep the card on your mind. If you lose your mind, you'll ruin everything.

• Because this is the last Saturday of the week, we'll do this special trick.

• People ask me what my favorite trick is. I hate my favorite trick!

• This trick goes back to the days when people who wore blue jeans worked.

• It's not much of a trick, but it makes you think. It makes you think it isn't much of a trick.

• I did this trick in Egypt and rolled them in the Nile. Some, however, didn't Cairo for it.

• Please don't tell me how it's done. It makes me nervous.

• I am not going to rush into the audience to have a card selected. Not for several reasons:

First, I may never return. The Magician's Union lost six performers that way last year. They were beaten to death with bags of popcorn by the enraged spectators.

Second, that lady in the balcony won't be able to see my smiling face, which she has come to depend upon.

And third, I ran the three-minute mile just before the show, so I don't need the exercise.

• No such power should be in the hands of one person.

• This is a fool-proof trick. I'm just the fool to prove it.

• As a rule, I don't do this trick in my regular show. I save it for my friends. But since I started doing it, I don't have any friends—so I'm going to do it for you right now.

• I could do those tricks before I could talk. I was sure glad when I got to be fifteen months old and could say, "Take a card."

• I'm letting you cut this rope for one reason. It's because I like you.

• I learned this trick from Professor Hook. Hook and I traveled together.

• An Indian magic word—Chief Chew Bubble Gum.

• I want you to think of every card in the deck except one. Now what card were you not thinking of? You don't understand. You *were* thinking of that card or you couldn't have named it. Oh, you can't name it because you aren't thinking of it?

Actually, it's not impossible to do. Merely think of every card in the deck except one. Now think of every one of the cards in the deck and subtract all the cards except one. The one card left over will be the one you are not thinking of.

(I, David Ginn, personally thought this up in 1965 while a student at the University of Georgia. I was happy to discover it as an entry in Gene Gordon's notebooks!)

• Am I responsible? Where I worked I was called responsible—for everything that went wrong!

• This next trick is one that has kept me in obscurity for many years.

• There are two ways to do this trick: the way I do it is the right way.

• When I bought this trick, they said that a child of three could do it. Well, I wish that three-year-old child was here to help me!

• During this trick, I go into a trance. Don't worry—you won't notice the difference.

• I could perform that trick if I wanted to—but I don't *want to.*

• Honestly, folks, this next trick frightens me out of my wits. But it's nice to get out once in a while.

In researching this book, I was discovered a distant relative who did magic too:. Here is my cousin Gordon Frederick Franklin, age 10 in 1887, taken in the studio photo of Wm. Kuhns & Sons, No. 37 Whitehall Street in Atlanta, Georgia.

Notice the change bag in his left hand and the custom taylored coat with 24 secret pockets. Very smart for his day. In fact, he had so many pockets in that coat, he couldn't find them all!

• My Chinese magician friend, Hun Wun, sent me the directions, but I couldn't read them. The only way I can read Chinese is when it's written in English.

• I'll mark this with a crayon—where I live they don't let us have anything sharp.

• If I don't accomplish this trick, I will be glad to accept five hundred dollars from any well-known charity.

• A hundred years from now, people will still be talking about this trick. It shows how dull life will be then.

• I performed this trick in front of four United

1902. Another picture of our Gordon Frederick Franklin, at age 25. He reminds me of the famous Frederick Eugene Powell, a well-known magic man in America.

The scraps of writing in very aged notes passed down to me are very difficult to read and decipher. Evidently, what magic he performed was purely for a hobby to amuse children at family gatherings and parties.

States Presidents, all at one time—in Mt. Rushmore, South Dakota.

• The next one will make you wonder—wonder what's on TV at this time.

• Gone with the Wand!

• This trick is so good that women frequently hurl their babies out of the balcony and strong men faint in the aisles from excitement.

• I'll say that magic word in Hindustani—INK A DINK A DOO. In English, that means "One good turn takes the whole blanket."

• *Someone stands up to leave.* Look at this. I haven't even finished the trick, and I'm getting a standing ovation.

• Before we start, I would like to state that I am not insured against accidents.

• *Chopper trick:* This is your lucky day. The operation is not going to cost you a cent.

• I once saw a magician do a trick where he pushed three white handkerchiefs through a tube and caused them to change color, just dyeing them. He commenced by saying, "I will now dye," and the audience cheered.

As I have only one handkerchief and no tube, I'll use my hand, which I have had for years. When I poke the scarf into the top of the hand, it emerges a much brighter color. Oh, there's nothing else in my hand. I'll bet you thought I used two hanks. You were quite right. I keep the other one in the secret pocket in my hand . . . here.

I'll show you how it's done. I start by grabbing a little air in my left hand, then poke the handkerchief inside and because of the pollution in the air, no one can see the scarf now. They think my hand is empty. If I push this one in at the top, the other one must come out at the bottom. But as I still have a handful of polluted air, you can't see the other handkerchief. When I go backstage, I'll blow away the smog, and I'll have no trouble getting my other handkerchief. It's that simple.

THE NEXT THREE PAGES consist of a break in the flow of this text, after which we will resume the rest of the book. I think you magic performers will find this side-trip interesting.

Gene Gordon's Pitch Act Intro

LONG AFTER the publication of *Magical Legacy,* I found this "Pitch Act Intro" among Gene's notes. It was not used in his book, so I will share it with you here. As Gene explained in his notes:

"Somebody on the Fantasy Island musical comedy show asked me to write an introduction to a pitch act. Since everybody has his own tricks to do with a pitch act, all they wanted was a talk to get into the act. It could not be claimed as original. Probably the best you could say is that Gene Gordon got this intro together from bits and pieces I have heard all my life."

I can hear Uncle Gene speaking these words:

Folks, if you'll all gather in a little closer . . . come on down in front . . . that's right— don't block the ones in the back . . . you will see the most amazing and amusing, educational and confusing exhibition of Hindu Scaperthemy ever shown before the public!

It's all FREE! So hurry, hurry, hurry! Step right up and see me do a miracle before your very eyes . . . and if you don't have 'very' eyes, there's something wrong with you!

I'm going to prove that the quickness of the hand completely deceives the euphraadonnafrazz and puzzles the faversham, especially on a foggy night.

You'll see the mollatoke becomes extremely fatalifay and remains in a completely candillated condition, at least until the frog-hunting season is over.

73

Now don't get the idea that I'm going to try and sell you something . . . not until I see somebody reach in his pocket.

I represent the famous Dr. Killum Medicine Company of Tombstone, Arizona, and our firm does not advertise on billboards, stagecoaches, in newspapers, or on signs of any description.

Instead, they hire me to introduce their product in your fair city—and to do it I am passing out to each and every one of you, *absolutely free of charge,* A BRAND NEW DOLLAR BILL!

That's right—come up close and get in on the big money . . . and it is big money I'm giving away. *(Wave big bill.)*

..ABSOLUTELY FREE OF CHARGE!

Now I know that if all of you don't get one of these dollar bills, there will be some sad people around here, and they'll just say there's a fake to it . . . so in order not to disappoint anybody, I'll just put the dollar bill back in my pocket and keep everybody happy.

What I'm really here for is not to sell any of Dr. Killum's Magic Powder for Mysterious Maladies, but merely to demonstrate how wonderful it is. It acts just like magic. In fact, you can do magic with just one application of this marvelous Dr. Killum's Magic Powder.

I'll show you. *(Do quick trick using powder to make it work).* And when I tell you some of the things that Dr. Killum's Magic Powder can cure, you'll say it's magic. It won't cure a broken arm, but you will find that it does everything else.

It will help you if you suffer from corns, bunions, rheumatism, asthma, hardening of the arteries, housemaid's knee, fallen arches, and juvenile delinquincy.

It makes a fine polish for black and tan shoes and is guaranteed to kill flies, fleas, mosquitoes, and that scourge of mankind, the boll weevil.

It will rid your house of rats, roaches, termites, and your wife's relatives. When mixed with 7-Up or Ginger-Ale, it makes a nice summer drink.

It's marvelous for adults—and if you don't suffer from adults, it can be used for other purposes.

It will remove spots and stains from your clothing—yes, it will even remove the cloth where the spot was!

It's great for reducing. I'll show you how good it is. *(Do trick where something shrinks.)*

As I said, I'm just here to advertise Dr. Killum's Magic Powder, but due to unknown reasons, the Company has failed to send me any expense money for the past two and a half years. This has forced me to raise money in order to keep from starving to death, so I have a little package here that I offer to each and every one of you who has the nerve, the courage, and the money to pay for it.

Not five dollars, not three dollars, not even one dollar, but just fifty cents will let you go home happy—and wise. Who'll be the first?

If you've never considered a comedy-magic pitch act, here's your start. Think W. C. Fields, and adapt.

9. No Easy Answers

DUANE LAFLIN, with the help of his wife Mary, has written many books on the performance of magic—stage, gospel, and comedy for family audiences. One of my personal favorites is *Duane's Comedy Lists*. With the permission of Duane and Mary, I have created this chapter largely from the "Hard to Answer Questions" chapter of that book, plus additional material I've heard or created.

Whether you employ all or some of these items, you will enjoy using these thought-questions to make people laugh and think. Having delivered most of this material in my own talks, for audiences both small and large, let me offer this advice:

Deliver these gags in a rapid-fire manner, not pausing too long between them. This produces a *think-laugh-think-laugh* pattern, which sometimes turns into applause.

• Why is the word *abbreviated* so long?

• Have you ever noticed that alarm clocks always go off when you're sleeping?

• When they ship styrofoam, what do they pack it in?

• And how does teflon stick to the pan?

• If somebody eats something he thinks has "gone bad," why does he always want *you* to taste it?

- When you dial the wrong number, why is it never busy?

- What do they call coffee breaks at the Lipton Tea Company?

- How do you know you have forgotten something if you can't remember what it is?

- Exactly how many pancakes would it take to shingle a doghouse? *(Thanks, Bob Brant)*

- How come a BROWN and WHITE cow eats GREEN grass and drinks CLEAR water, then turns around and gives YELLOW butter and WHITE milk and CHOCOLATE on Thursdays?

- In the newspaper obituary columns, how come people always die in alphabetical order?

- Why is a TV set just one piece?

- And why do you park in a driveway and drive on a parkway?

- Think about this: if your knees bent the other way, what would a chair look like?

- What is the difference between maybe and maybe not?

- If a person lives at the end of a one-way street, how does he ever move?

- When you look up the word *redundant* in the dictionary, does it say, "see redundant?"

• Statistics say that every fifth child born in the world is Chinese. So if you already have four children, what language will your fifth child speak?

• If your nose runs and your feet smell, are you built upside-down?

• What is the difference between occasional irregularity and regular irregularity?

• If most auto accidents happen within five miles of home, why don't more people move?

• And have you ever considered this: why do they call it Rush Hour when all the cars move so slowly?

• If it's made of styrofoam, we call it a styrofoam CUP. If it's made of paper, we call it a paper CUP. So why, when it's made of *plastic,* do we call it a GLASS?

• Do fish have necks?

• Do penguins have knees?

• Do teeth sweat?

• You know that number you're supposed to call if you lose your credit card? Tell me, why is it printed on the BACK of the card?

• If a store stays open 365 days a year, 24 hours a day—why do they put locks on the doors?

• When you see a fly on the ceiling, how did it get there? Was it flying upside-down all the time, then landed up? Or did it do a back flip at the last moment?

• And tell me—how do flies sleep on the ceiling without falling down?

• Consider this: if you went back in time, you could conceivably alter the course of history, but you wouldn't. Because you didn't. *(Thanks, Joel Achenbach.)*

• Do birds of prey say grace before meals?

• If *pro* is the opposite of *con,* then is *progress* the opposite of CONGRESS? *(Thanks, Charlie Sable.)*

• Here's one I bet you've all wondered about: Where do Dracula's clothes go when he turns into a bat?

• Why does everyone know you have bad breath before you do when your nose is less than one inch from your mouth?

Thanks to Charlie Sable for the next three:

• Did you know that the word RACECAR spelled backwards—is RACECAR?

• And if your temperature is 99.66, it looks the same upside-down as right-side up?

• Also, have you considered that DESSERTS spelled backwards is STRESSED? Which is what you'll get if you eat too many desserts!

• Does water sink or float?

• Do mosquitoes dream?

• How many buffaloes would it take to fill the Grand Canyon?

• And why do roaches always turn over on their backs when they die?

• If you melt dry ice in a swimming pool, can you dive in without getting wet?

• Where does the white go when snow melts?

• What color of hair do they put on the driver's license of a bald-headed man?

• If a man writes a book titled *How To Be A Total Failure* and he doesn't sell a single copy—is he a success?

• FINALLY: Everyone says that falling bread lands butter-side down. And they say a falling cat will always land on its feet. So what would happen if you buttered a piece of bread . . . strapped it to a cat's back . . . and dropped the cat off a ten-story building?

I'D REALLY LIKE TO KNOW!

10. Health

SECOND ONLY to talk about the weather is talk about health. Don't ask "How are you?" unless you expect an answer sometimes! My mom once had a button which read: "Have you seen my operation yet?" That gave her the opening to tell of her surgery. People are always talking about doctors, surgery, and health in general. Capitalize on it! Joke about it! Have fun with health without getting too clinical. Sometimes, it's better to laugh than to worry.

• I still practice weight lifting—everytime I stand up.

• A cold is both positive and negative—sometimes the eyes have it and sometimes the nose.

- You should meet our doctor. He's the village cut-up!

- How am I feeling? Just like a window: I'm full of pain!

- Some hospital. They have a sign that says "NO CHILDREN ALLOWED" in the Maternity Ward.

- A hiccup is merely a message from departed spirits.

- The barber told me to use that tonic, and my hair would come in heavy. Only one hair grew, but it weighed eight pounds.

- The doctor said his operation would cost $2000 to open him up and $2000 to close. So he saved $2000 by pulling himself together. . . . He had his appendix taken out, and his father said, "That's enough out of you!"

- You've heard of the Hair Club for Men? I'm starting a similar club for hairless dogs.

- I use the wonder drug—Selfadenial.

- Uncle Ben was a doctor here, but he moved to Egypt and became a Cairo-practor.

- I used to have an inferiority complex, but my psychiatrist said I didn't have a complex. I was really inferior.

- I'm so full of penicillin that every time I sneeze, I cure someone.

- Nurse, this boy may need artificial recreation.

Uncle Nevil Duff, in 1894, was a ventriloquist, and here is one of his hand-made vent figures, to my knowledge the only Siamese Twins dummy every constructed.

My grandmother Ida Grey recalled seeing Nevil Duff perform in the early 1900s at a family picnic.

"It was the silliest thing you've ever seen," she said, *"making those dolls talk and knocking their heads all together. Some of the children even thought they were alive!"*

11. Kid Helpers

A KID AT HEART. That's what I am. That fact makes me a better children's entertainer because I understand what children like and want and feel.

That's why I am able to play creatively with my kid audiences during my 300 yearly school shows while maintaining direction and control.

When I say funny things to a child or about a child during my shows, I feel that the kids *know* I am playing, teasing, jiving, making kidbiz fun. It's our kind of entertainment—nothing out of order, nothing wrong, just playing with funny words.

"You have to be a comedian to play kidshows," Gene once wrote, "and most comedians are mostly children. That's why comedians live longer than most people. You have to have a youthful view to live in this world today. If you don't, you will die early from depression."

That bears out my contention that you cannot do children's shows without some comedy, at least not successfully. I can think of no successful kidshow worker who performs without lots of funny stuff.

Here are some lines that Gene, David, and a few other friends—including you—might use to create laughter with child helpers on stage or off.

• I want to thank you for making this show impossible.

• *Say to two kids on stage:* One of you stand here—and the other two come with me.

• *To a girl:* What a beauty! May I say that ever since you came up here, no other girl has been on my mind. Are you married? Is your husband here with you? No? Where is he? Oh, you say he's home with the kids? How old are you? Only eight? Why, you don't look a day over five! How do you keep looking so young? What's your secret?

• Don't you dare laugh like that again, or I'll change you into a rabbit.

• Hold them in front of your nose. Is that your nose?

• *To child:* I hope I look as well as you do, when I get to be your age.

• *Boy and girl helpers:* You can be the Hero, and you can be the She-ro.

• *To child helper:* Just hold this above your head—about 15 feet!

• **GENE GORDON KIDBIT No. 1:** From a teacher or the principal, I would get the name of a girl seated on the aisle. Let's say her name was Ruth Harrison.

When I went into the audience to have a card, horse, or pineapple selected, I would stop, look at the girl and say, "You are an exact twin of a girl in my elementary school graduating class. Her name was Ruth Harrison." Everyone around her would gasp and say, "That was *her* name!" I would act amazed, and she would laugh with delight or perhaps put on a shy act. At any rate, it always got a good reaction.

Which one would you pick for a child helper on stage? If your show was in 1894, you might have picked Hassie Mae Meadows, left (my maternal grandmother), or her sister Eva.

- *Jokingly to boy:* Never walk in front of the star.

- What's your name again, George? I forgot.

- *To kid not holding prop up:* What happened? Your hand fall asleep?

- I just love children. I went to school with them.

- Did your parents ever ask you to run away from home?

- One time I accidentally cut off a boy's ear. I told him I was sorry, but I don't think he heard me.

- **GENE GORDON KIDBIT No. 2:** At the end of a trick, as I dismissed a small boy and a small girl, I would give the girl a jumbo dollar bill as a souvenir.
Then I would look at the boy, as if wondering what to give him. Finally I would say, "I'm going to give you, George, a gift that is the best of all. I'm going to give you—Autumn (the girl)! I want you to take her home with you and tell your mother, 'This is the girl I'm going to marry!'"
I just rolled with the variety of reactions to this gag for a moment or two, then I finally gave the boy a jumbo bill and thanked him too.

- Can I count on you? Oh, I can. *Tap your fingers on boy's head.* ONE, TWO, THREE, FOUR . . .

- Answer the phone, will you? What, it's not ringing? Well, why wait until the last minute?

- *Chopper trick.* A boy stuck both hands in, and they were chopped off. I've been wondering ever since how he feels. . . . Seriously, folks, I want you people out there to laugh a lot during this trick. This young man is just dying to make you laugh.

- Do you like candy? *Hand child a small paper bag.* Good, here's a bag to keep it in.

- *Kid holding prop.* Raise down with it and up a little lower.

- *To little girl:* Do you make faces at little boys, or do you make eyes at them?

- Do you have those little white things in your head that bite? What? You don't have any teeth?

- I'm going to borrow one of Tarzan's lions and let you take it home for a pet.

- **GENE GORDON KIDBIT No. 3:** *Use this in any trick where a small girl will assist you. All you need is a vanishing cane set to change into one or two silks. Do this:*

> You folks may wonder why I chose this young lady to help me. It is because I could see she has an air of mystery about her. I think she's a MAGIC GIRL! Let's find out.
> She could probably fly through the air if she wanted to. Maybe she could fly on this solid cane of mine and give you folks a good show. Just like riding a magical skateboard or surfboard!
> Tell you what: I'll hold out the cane out like this *(hold it horizontally),* and count to three. On three, you grab the cane with both hands, hop onto it, and ride it through the air around the auditorium, right over the heads of the audience. Don't forget to come back, since it's my cane, after all.
> Just fly or float right to the back of the room, then come back. Whatever you do, don't let go of the cane. Now, which way will you fly first? Up this side or that side? Make up your mind. Here we go: one, two, three!

As the girl grabs for the cane, step lightly back and change the cane into two silks. You can time the vanish as you watch her movements.

Hey, what goes on here? I can see that you do have MAGIC POWERS, but I didn't think you would play any of your tricks on me. Shame on you! I guess you will be just the one to help me do this next trick!

• This boy has everything. He should be guaranteed.

• *Little boy and girl standing beside each other.* Don't they make a lovely couple?

• Your name? Albert? A boy named Albert can't be all bad.

• Don't be nervous. I know this is the first time you have appeared before me.

• I'm going to give him a watch as soon as he learns to tell time.

• That look of disbelief on his face is something that will haunt me the rest of my days.

• What year were you born? That was a good year for boys.

• Say, I know you. Your name is Herman Himplesweitzer. Why are you here under an assumed name?

• Don't bite your nails. Don't you know what happened to a girl named Venus de Milo? *(Adults laugh at this.)*

• Turn around and face the audience. He has a funny idea where his face is.

• You are only ten? Why, at your age I was twelve.

• May I have the assistance of some young man who is willing to give his life in the cause of science?

• Stand there—right over the transporter beam.

• Some of you are Boy Scouts, Cub Scouts, Girl Scouts, Brownies and other cookies.

• What's your name? It doesn't really matter. I'll just call you Clarence.

• He used to be a bottle baby. Then he reached the age of nine, pushed the cork out, and escaped from the bottle.

A 1950s birthday party for Cousin Rita Miller, Arlington, Georgia. That's Rita in the foreground left, next to brother Otis Jr. who is shirtless, followed by Frankie Miller (my brother-in-law), and my future wife, Lynne Miller, standing, who is seriously examining a noise-making blow-out party favor.

• **GENE GORDON KIDBIT No. 4:** When a kid does a good job of assisting you, stick a peel-off gold star on his forehead. Tell him that if he keeps it on for a week, it will bring him good luck—he will get a free holiday from school next Saturday!

- *Look at boy's hands, shake head.* I see you have been walking on your hands again.

- I think it would be nice if you stood by the door when the show is over, and everybody could show their appreciation by giving you a pat on the head.

- *To helpful boy:* I'll see that you get a merit badge at your next patrol meeting.

- *To little girl:* Would you marry me? I want to make my wife jealous.

- You understand, of course, this is only a summer childhood romance. We don't know how we'll feel about each other next summer.

- Your name is Henry—now don't you forget that.

- Somehow I get the feeling I'm an out-patient and you are in charge of me.

- Are your parents here? Well, do a good job— make them proud of you.

- Have we ever met before? No? Then how do you know it's me? *(Yes, it's old—but it still plays!)*

- You must have missed your nap today. You probably slept right through it.

- Will the lady who has the lucky number come up and take this boy for her prize.

• In all my years on stage, Mary, I have never had a better audience assistant than you. And now I must bid you *adieu.* That means goodbye in French, the language they speak in France. *Adieu, adieu, mon cheri.* Parting is such sweet sorrow. Think of me, when you think of our time together here on stage, at this *one moment in time,* when the earth and time stood still, when we were strangers on the shore, when we were having the time of our lives, when nothing really mattered except the card trick you so lovingly helped me to accomplish. Think of me, everytime you see the Jack of Spades, and I will think of you, each time I see the Queen of Hearts. For you, Mary, are the undisputed Queen of My Heart. *Pause a moment.* NEXT VOLUNTEER!

It's a joke—let's give my friend Mary a huge round of applause!

12. Family Matters

MY SECOND FAVORITE audience, beyond children, is the family audience. It's great fun to perform at a family night dinner with parents and kids present. I play a lot to the children, but the parents have the added experience of seeing their children react to my comedy magic.

Things happen in family life that kids and parents always remember. Funny things. Not so funny things.

Some families have running jokes that go on for years. The family that jokes together feels a sense of companionship and closeness. Playful teasing and joshing create a sense of family love, sometimes between family members who have a hard time saying "I love you."

Keep in mind we are talking of healthy fun-making here, *not* making destructive fun of a child. Do or say nothing that humiliates or pokes fun at the child as a valuable person.

Personally, I seldom jokingly tease people I don't like. And some of the friends I do tease are the ones I like the most. If it's a friend or family member who can banter it back to me, all the better. That means we're both having the pleasure of playing with words designed to stimulate each other's thoughts.

What's funny about your family and friends?

- I'm going to speak on trade relations because I have some relations I'd like to trade.

- We have all period furniture at home. We have it for a period, then they come and get it.

- As a child, I slept in a bed nine feet long. That's a lot of bunk.

- Where there's a will — there's a lot of disappointed relatives.

- I came from a very poor family. They couldn't afford to have children, so our neighbors had me. Eleven kids in our family. We were so poor we had to wear each other's clothes. It wasn't funny. I had ten sisters!

- Money is a relative thing. Every time I get some, here comes one of my relatives.

- I was always an insecure child. I don't even know what I want to do when I grow up.

• My sister used to dye her own hair. One week it was red. Next week it was blonde. You might say she had a convertible top.

• My grandfather used to drink gallons of water, then sit back in his rocking chair. Just sit there and slosh around all day.

• He comes from an old family—so old it's been condemned.

• My uncle is working on a universal solvent that will dissolve anything. I asked him: "If it will dissolve anything, what will you keep it in?"

Good family reading @ 1930-40. Notice that father not only sits to read to the group, but mother is left standing and holding a huge baby in this family of seven children.

• Home is where you hang your head.

• My uncle was so clean he took six showers a day. When he died, the funeral procession went through the car wash on the way to the cemetery.

• I live in a total electric house. Everything is charged.

• Keeping peace in a large family requires many things: patience, love, understanding—and at least two television sets with remote controls.

13. Doing Shows

ALL THESE LINES have to do with performing on stage and what happens before and after. Sometimes it's fun to "make fun" of what you're doing or going to do . . . just for the fun of it, which can even be funny.

• Last night I stopped the show. I was the last act.

• One night while I was doing my stunts, the roof of the theatre collapsed. That's one time I really brought down the house.

• I enjoy putting on floor shows. I used to be a vacuum cleaner salesman.

• I had to share my dressing room with a gorilla. The manager came down and apologized for putting us together. I said, "Oh, that's all right," and he said, "I wasn't talking to you."

• I won't criticize the orchestra, but last night a waiter dropped a tray of dishes and six couples got up to dance.

• When I played Siberia, people went down in the salt mines who didn't even work there.

• *Looking into orchestra pit.* Looks like an open grave.

• Are you in show business? No? Then get your elbow off my stage!

• After my act I sat down, and everybody said it was the best thing I did.

• Your committee hired me because they believe there's nothing like a good magician . . . and I'm nothing like a good magician.

• I have had the honor of appearing before all the crowned heads of Europe and some very peculiar people from Lackawanna (*name small town*).

• I haven't made a free appearance since the nurse held me up to the window.

• They threw a tomato at one of the performers. Boy, was my face red!

• I'm doing this show for a good cause—'cause I need the money.

• During the committee's congratulations, a boy came up and said, "The show was lousy." One of the committeemen said, "That boy isn't quite bright. He doesn't know what he's saying. He only repeats what he hears other people say."

• I planned on having an escape artist here today, but he was tied up.

• I'd like to tell you how glad I am to be here, only I'm not sure yet.

• My last show was in a church. At the finish I took a bow, backed up and fell into the baptismal pool. Fortunately, there was no water in it, or I'd be a Baptist now.

14. Outdoor Shows

EVERY PERFORMER imagines show-biz as a complete stage with curtains, a fine sound system, magnifcent scenery, and beautiful lighting. Unfortunately, performing conditions are seldom perfect, and many of us end up doing outdoor shows at times. Making fun of the outdoor situation allows you to have fun, sometimes when it's not such fun.

• It's a pleasure to be working here in the great outdoors . . . among the trees and below the sky . . . where birds fly overhead and greet us with beautiful singing and little deposits.

• I was going to use a big, colorful silk scarf for this trick, except the wind blew it away.

• Ah—to work outdoors with the babbling of a little brook in the background. Brook? Where are you? I'd like for that girl named Brook to stand up and babble for us!

• It's the great outdoors! Where men are men, women are women, and trees smell like pine sap!

• How do you like this carpet? *(Indicate the grass.)* I bet it didn't cost 25 dollars a square yard!

• Today I was going to magically produce 14 doves, 22 parakeets, an owl, a cockatoo, and a live buzzard during this show—then I looked up at all those trees they'd love to fly into—and I settled for the rabbit!

• Gee, I love this natural air-conditioning!

• I love trees. I know all about them. That's a pine tree. It's full of sap. That's a maple. I can tell by its leaves. That's a dogwood. I can tell by its bark.

Outdoors at Stone Mountain, Georgia, @ 1909-10. My mother's family, left to right: Edwin & Hassie Mathews (my grandparents), Noah Matthews, Van Dora Matthews Glover, Emma Corroll Matthews, William T. (Billy) Matthews, Sarah Ellen Garner Matthews, and "Uncle Oscar" H. Matthews, the doctor who delivered me!

- Here we all are, with the sky as our roof. If it rains, we'll know our roof leaks!

- Since we're oudoors, remember that you can laugh and applaud as LOUD as you want. It won't bother me!

- *Working on ground.* Did anyone mop this stage? How do they expect me to tap dance on this? Guess I'll have to do magic!

- How do you like this, folks—my offstage is that clump of bushes!

- *Working next to tree:* I'm allergic to bees. They give me hives. Sorry about that. I went out on a limb for that one. I know, time to branch out. . . . Okay, I'm a sap. I think I'll leaf! *(Steve Taylor)*

- Palm a rubber production shoe. Hold up a large rock and pretend to pull the shoe out of it. Remark, "Hey—there's a shoe in my rock!"

- *Audience sitting on ground.* Now I want each of you to stay in your reserved seat during the show.

- *Swat at fly or bee.* Say—who opened the door and let that bee into the theater?

- There's a buzzard sitting up in that tree watching the show. He reminds me of a New York film critic.

- So this is where fresh air comes from!

15. Government and Taxes

THIS ISN'T WHAT the govern-meant. Somehow, something has gone wrong . . . and we gotta keep picking on it, making fun of it, so someday maybe we can get it right.

• Yes, I am proud to be paying taxes to the government. However, I could be just as proud for half the money.

• A fine is a tax you pay for doing wrong. A tax is a fine you pay for doing right.

Sgt. Frank Ginn and Helen Ginn at home in Atlanta @ 1945. World War II was still going on, and David Ginn did not yet exist!

• I just got back from Washington, where half the people are waiting to be discovered and the other half are afraid they will be.

• If they ever tax brains, what a refund I'll get!

• Crime wouldn't pay if the government ran it.

• You pay a luxury tax on your billfold, an income tax on the stuff you put in it, and a sales tax every time you take anything out of it.

• While it seems silly to mention it now, this country was founded as a protest against taxation.

• I'm going to retire next year and let the government become self-supporting.

• That baby crying must be a Democrat (or Republican). He thinks it's time for a change.

• It's getting harder and harder to support the government in the style to which it is accustomed.

• Political plums don't grow from seeds. They are the result of clever grafting.

• One thing you can say about our politicians: They are running our government like nobody's business.

• A man owes it to himself to become successful. Once successful, he owes it to the IRS.

• *Here's a quote you might enjoy:* "One worthless man is a disgrace. Two useless men become a law firm. And three or more . . . are called Congress." — John Adams

16. Sense and Nonsense

THERE WAS A TIME when it was funny to say things that didn't make sense purely for a laugh.

The idea was simple: since the utterance made no sense whatsoever, it was funny because it was nonsense, though the casual listener didn't realize the non-sense of it, the sense being that you were speaking nonsense just to amuse yourself or others "in" on the joke.

I'm not so sure that that time has passed. Inserting such nonsense in your patter from time to time can produce laughs, or at the very least, offer misdirection. So if any of this makes sense to you . . . the sense would be to use it.

• The big bopper walks before day.

• Well, send me off to the dude ranch.

• Remember—few are called . . . but some are.

• Hair-brained as it sounds, I think it won't buy gasoline.

• Say when you will, you are, you could be as strong as nothing. And remember the words of the poet—"Nothing matters and what if it did?"

• Don't let anyone pull the wool over your sheepskin.

Ophelia Hamilton Dent, a distant cousin, insists I quote her:
"This chapter is full of plain, pure nonsense, and whether you have read it or not already, I strongly suggest you do not read any more of it now. In fact, do not even waste your time reading this paragraph. I didn't!"

- I wish you could see what I heard.

- Now wait a year! *(Like "wait a minute.")*

- I'll be left there. *(Instead of right there).*

- When the sands of time meet the salt of the earth, you'll have a grainy picture tube.

- Remember: COMEDY is no laughing matter.

- Now stand tall and watch the tide roll into the nearest parking meter.

- Well, bless my popcorn popper.

- So, you're the one with the who-where-what-not!

• Remember—Bonie Maronie Eats Macaroni!

• Just give me a dog that won't eat chocolate.

• That guy knows more in his little finger than my brain thinks of yesterday.

• Remember the immortal words of Boswell, who said centuries ago, "Dark happiness is the sinister intent of the chocolate lover in a fudge factory."

• No matter why you did, whoever said not to— didn't know how you should.

• Remember, buttered elephant ears make great pancakes.

• Do you think all the gold in California would buy all the tea in China?

• Never buy squirt soap out of a bubble gum machine.

• *And I hope you'll enjoy these three new songs I heard recently on the radio:*

Δ I'm Dancing Tonight with My Face All Scratched 'cause the Girl in My Arms Has a Beard

Δ I Made a Suitcase Out of the Alligator that Ate You Up

Δ Goodnight, My Love, Sweet Dreams, My Love, In Dreams You Don't Have Bad Breath, My Love

17. People . . . Who Need People

EVERYONE IN THIS chapter is not real. If I didn't have a better place to put it and the line involved human beings, it landed here.

Like a line? Use it. Sorta like a line, change it. Make it suit your personality and situation to make people laugh at themselves and/or you.

• Ya know, other people are bothered by juvenile delinquents. Me? I get the adult ones.

• He's laughing, but he's miserable.

• One reason many people live in the past is simple—it's cheaper.

• I read in the newspaper that a sink hole mysteriously appeared in Peachtree Street today. But don't worry. Police are looking into it. *(Thanks, Steve Taylor.)*

• Some men are like worms. They crawl around until some chick picks them up.

• It's only natural that a politician won the outlying districts. He was out lying to all of them.

• He's all right in his place, but they haven't dug it yet.

• I asked a guy in the elevator what time it was, and he said he left his watch upstairs.
I asked, "Aren't you afraid it'll run down?"
He said, "No—we have a winding staircase!"
(Bruce "Sparkles"Johnson)

• Lincoln once walked nine miles to borrow a book from the library, so now they close the libraries on his birthday.

• I know girls aren't perfect, but they are the only opposite sex we have.

• He's a perfectionist. He takes great pains and gives them to others.

• She sang for the Gas Company commercials. Everytime she sang, 3000 people got gas.

• I've got an inquisitive nephew. He took his nose apart to see what made it run.

• I called him aside, . . . and left him there.

• I cured my nephew of biting his nails. I made him wear shoes.

• He's an athlete and has the feet to prove it.

• My uncle was a nervous man. No wonder, he worked in a dynamite factory. One day he went all to pieces.

• He got a suspended sentence—they hung him.

• He's going out of his mind, and his mind is glad he's leaving.

• He loves crowds. He's a pick-pocket.

• He has that lean look. He's always looking for something to lean on.

• My uncle was run over by a steam roller. He's in the hospital, flat on his back, in Rooms 222 . . . 223 . . . and 224.

• He knows all the answers. It's the questions that fool him.

• Who was St. Matthew, St. Mark, or St. Peter? What? You think Peter was a rabbit?

• I have nothing against young people. I just hope my nephew doesn't become one.

• He'll stick in his oars, but never offer to row.

• In Africa, some of the native tribes practice a strange custom of beating the ground with clubs and uttering wild, blood-curdling yells. Anthropologists call this a form of self-expression. In America, we call it golf.

• I don't know what the professor died of, but it wasn't anything serious.

• I shoot golf in the low seventies. If it gets any colder, I quit.

• He has a strange hobby. He sits in a corner and collects dust.

• He's so uninhibited, and his head is so uninhabited.

Lorene Smith traveled with three girlfriends by car from south Georgia to the New York World's Fair in 1939, the trip of a lifetime. Here Lorene stands atop the hood of a car with another friend, "cutting up" at age 23. Five years later she married Ivey Miller, and the two eventually become the parents of my wife Lynne.

• For every curve she's got, there's an angle that goes with it.

• Excuse me? Have you ever had an out-of-body experience? I mean—have you lost your mind?

• Job was a smart baby. He talked when he was less than 24 hours old. In fact, the Bible says that Job cursed the day he was born.

• I can tell by your tie that you have a funny sense of humor.

• No man is good enough for her. She may be right. She may be left.

• He's in a class with gamblers, crooks and used car dealers.

My father-in-law, Ivey A. Miller, @ 1938-39, down on the farm in Moultrie, Georgia.

One good automobile pose deserves another.

• He's a funny guy. I wish I had half the wit he does. But that would make me a . . . oh, nevermind! *(Steve Taylor)*

• Talk about lazy! He is so lazy that he put coffee grounds in his mustache and drank hot water.

• *Audience man asleep.* You'll have to excuse him. He missed his nap today. Slept right through it. You know, I wish he'd learn a trade so we'd know what kind of work he was out of!

• In the old days, there used to be things that people didn't talk about. Now they talk about nothing else!

• I asked him if he liked bathing beauties, but he said he had never bathed any. Now there's a law: you can't change your clothes on the beach. It doesn't bother him. He changes his clothes on the bus going to the beach.

• As a child, I was so thin it took two of me to make a shadow.

• He was an athlete in school. Played on the tiddley-wink team. He played left tiddle.

• Everybody's so impressed with the Queen of England. What's so wonderful? She got the job through relatives.

• She says she likes antiques, but they have to be up to date and modern.

• He's got a strange hobby—goes to every wedding he hears about. After the ceremony, he is one of the first to rush up and give the bride a long, tender kiss. Then both sides try and figure out who he is.

• His black eye came from a guided muscle.

• I'm one of his friends. I'm in the minority.

• He never found himself, and when he does, he'll be sorry.

• She wanted a dress to wear around the house. I don't think they make dresses that big.

• I'll never forget the first time I met him.

• He'll never live to be as old as he looks.

May 11, 1933. The Camp Fire Girls surprised my mother, Helen Matthews, on her 12th birthday. She's kneeling with the cake.

- I can tell character when I see it—and he's a character if I ever saw one.

- He can resist anything except temptation.

- Fifty people picketed City Hall demanding something be done about air pollution. Then they jumped into 47 cars and drove home.

- He's a legend in his own mind.

- He's a fugitive from the law of average. He's average, though—he's got ten toes just like anyone else—two on one foot and eight on the other.

- Last boy she kissed said he'd never use his lips to eat with again.

• He's an undertaker—the last man to let you down.

• I'll never forget the first time I met him. It was in a nightmare.

• *To talkative audience person:* I give up—who's working his head?

• Excuse me. I didn't hear you because I was talking.

• She just ignored me—and I can't stand ignorance.

• He used to attend a medical school. He was one of the subjects.

• My attorney just went to work for a new law firm: DEWEY, CHEATAM, AND HOWE.

• He threw himself onto the ground, but he missed.

• Who, Hershel? He's a strange fellow . . . goes to group therapy alone.

Answer to Gene Gordon Quiz, p. 16-17

Now for the answer you've been waiting for. The picture on the LEFT page (page 16) is Gene Gordon at age six months. The picture on the right (page 17) is a picture of—not David Ginn— but my mother, Helen Matthews Ginn, at about the same age!

18. Cannibals Are People Too

AUTUMN AND DENA, daughter and friend at age 12, were reading this joke book, so I picked it up when they weren't looking. I read the first joke on this list, loved it, and used it a number of times. When I told it at the FCM California Convention during a lecture, several people shared other cannibal jokes with me afterwards. They were so funny I couldn't write them down fast enough. Here they are—plus a lot more.

• Did you hear about the cannibal who had a wife and eight children?

• One night the cannibal stayed out playing cards with his friends. When he came home late for supper, his wife gave him the cold shoulder.

• Then there was the cannibal who went on a diet. He only eats thin people. *(Bruce Johnson)*

• In fact, cannibalism is even recorded in the Bible. It says Two Corinthians Ate One. (II Cor. 8:1). —*Bruce Johnson again*

Mary and Duane Laflin offered these four:

• My uncle is a cannibal. He has been living on us for 20 years!

- FIRST CANNIBAL: "We've just captured a movie star."
SECOND CANNIBAL: "Great! I was hoping for a good ham sandwich!"

- Why should you stay calm when you meet a cannibal? You don't want to get him into a stew!

- What do cannibals have for lunch? Baked BEINGS!

Then my Morton, Illinois, magic friend Jeff Dickerson jumped on the cannibal bandwagen and added all of these—

- A cannibal is lucky. He can have his Kate and Edith too.

- His favorite Chinese dish is Moo Goo Guy in a Pan.

- His favorite seafood choice is broiled fisherman platter.

- His favorite Sunday dinner is roast Chuck.

- He really prefers a lunch of beans and Frank

- He gets excited about finger foods.

- He enjoys a light lunch of chef in a salad.

- He likes to stop where they serve truck drivers.

- When the missionaries arrived, he got a taste of religion.

• He always enjoys a businessman's lunch.

Enough, Jeff, I think you could go on and on. Okay, just three more of yours, then we finish this chapter:

• Did you hear about the little cannibal who was sent home from school? He kept buttering up the teacher.

• Then there was the cannibal who hoped to catch a politician so he could have a bologna sandwich.

• Finally, the cannibal hung his head and announced, "My wife makes wonderful soup. Sure will miss her!"

Well, I thought I'd finished the chapter, but Steve Taylor had to add his share of cannibal humor:

• What did the cannibal say when he was cooking a clown? "Something smells funny!"

• A missionary found his buddy cooking in a pot. Looking sad, he asked, "What's eating you?" *Maybe, Steve, it should be, WHO's eating you!*

• A boy cannibal said to his mother, "What—soup again?" The mom replied, "Quiet, Son, eat your STU!"

• Everytime I eat dinner with cannibals, the evening goes to pot!

• "Hey, Mom, I switched lunches with the bully at school," said the little cannibal. "What did you get in the trade?" she asked. "A knuckle sandwich!"

• A cannibal is one person who is allowed to eat with his elbows on the table.

Just a few more thoughts—

• The cannibal's name was Will Rogers. He never met a man he didn't like.

• I wonder if cannibals ever get fed up with people?

• A cannibal went to dinner on a cruise ship. The water asked if he'd like to see the menu. "No," the cannibal replied, "just the passenger list."

• He used to be a cannibal—often had his friends for dinner.

• Have you read the Betty Crocker cookbook for cannibals? It's called *How to Serve Man.*

• The little cannibal said to his mother, "Mom, can I eat my sandwich with my fingers?" She said, "No, son, eat your sandwich FIRST—then, *eat your fingers.*"

19. Banquets and More

RAISE YOUR HAND if you've been to a banquet lately? Come on! We all love banquet food! It's such an adventure, from wonderful to "Where's the Alka-Seltzer?" It's so much fun to have everyone seated in his or her proper place, all dressed up, using good manners, saying gracious things. Nothing to make fun of here—or, is there?

• I just love banquets. It's so neat to have a real tablecloth to wipe your hands on!

• I have a question, as long as we're here at the banquet: If you're right-handed, how come they always put the fork on your left? That really bothers me!

• I could see my face in my plate. It looked like I had a beard made out of green beans!

• How many here ate your entire meal with your napkin in your lap? Raise your hands. Okay, how many dropped your napkin on the floor at least once? Hands up. Okay. How many did not use your napkin at all? Wipe your mouths!

• Okay, how many have your shoes off under the table?

• How did you enjoy the crabmeat jello?

• I love banquets like this. It sure beats eating diet bars!

• I've been to hundreds of banquets. How do you think I learned to eat mashed potatoes without using my hands? Really, I wonder—how many of you at home make little rows in your mashed potatoes and plant your black-eyed peas in the rows before you eat them?

• Wow—this sure beats sitting in my three million dollar mansion eating dinner alone!

• It's great to be eating here with all you folks. Kinda reminds me of the boarding house back in college!

• Was that apple pie good! You know what they say—an apple pie a day keeps the doctor away . . . or something like that!

• What great food! In fact, I saw one guy at the dessert table loading up three pies in a doggie bag!

• I sure love that butter-flavored ice cream they have on each table.

• By the way, did any of you see that cute little gerbil running around the salad bar?

• This is the first banquet I've ever attended that was catered with TV dinners!

My best friend as a kid, Steve "Buck" Gibson and me, David Ginn, on my front porch @ 1951-52. We're all dressed up with someplace to go . . . probably church.

OVERLEAF: From my mother's family, a Garner family reunion @ 1910, somewhere near the Stone Mountain / Mountain Park area, where I actually live now. Boy, if I had a time machine, I'd go back and do a show for them right now!

• When you're finished with your meal, please write your evaluation on your paper napkin and leave it in your water glass. Thank you.

• All right. Before we start the show, let's have a show of hands: How many of you *cleaned your plate?*

• It's great to be here at the baseball banquet with mom and apple pie!

• I want each of you to pick up a spoon, knife, or fork—and on the count of three, drop it on the table. One, two, three! (BAM!) Hey—*heavy metal!*

• Before the show, would all of you please pass your plates to the left, your silverware to the right, your glasses and cups across, and hold your napkins!

• Don't worry about your dishes. Just leave them on the table, and Mom will take care of them just like at home.

• On the way in, I saw a waitress carrying a plate with her thumb on a piece of steak. I told her I didn't think that was a proper way to bring in the food. She said she knew it didn't look good, but she didn't want the steak to fall on the floor again. *(Thanks, Jim Kleefeld)*

• We shall have no napkins tonight, but fear not— now and then, during the course of the meal, a wooly dog will pass among you. *(Sounds like Gene Gordon to me. —DG)*

20. It's A Dog's Life

AT THE UNIVERSITY of Georgia I wrote a campus humor column for the school newspaper, *The Red and Black.* "It's a Dog's Life" referred to UGA's "bulldog" symbol, "bulldog" or "dog" being a nickname for anyone connected with the University. Most often the material was true—things I had seen, been told about, been called about, sent notes and mail about. When I ran short of funnies, I'd ask and call and, yes, even make them up! Listen, folks, I had two deadlines each week!

So, if you're in a position to work for teenagers or college students, here are some lines and gags that are at least 20 years old . . . but recyclable with a word change here and there. Why, I'd certainly use them!

• English class comment: "Until I got into English 101, I thought *Roget's Thesaurus* was some kind of dinosaur!"

• *Math class.* Do I like logarithms? No, those Hungarian dishes give me indigestion.

• *Overheard, student to student.* I can arrange for you to take out this beautiful girl, but there's one catch. She's not an interesting talker.

• That class was so easy that the only difference between being there and doing nothing is that when you're there, they take roll.

• *Sorority house girl to visitor.* We don't use the carpeted steps very often. If we do, they get dirty.

• *English class.* The teacher asked, "What was Agamemnon's first name?" and I answered her. "It was KING!"

• *Girl to girl.* Is he really that good-looking? *Reply:* No, it's just that odd people appeal to me.

• *Teacher response.* No, you may not ask a question. Questions are the best way of stalling.

• Do I have many hard exams next week? No, just one in each course!

• *Conversation really overheard.* I had to miss class because I had pneumonia. *Oh, double?* No, single—I'm not married.

• *Another conversation.* Do you enjoy Picasso? *Answer.* No, actually I prefer pistachio.

• There's no point in reading *TV Guide* if you don't have a television set.

• *Yeah, Right Department.* If I go to a movie right now, it will refresh my mind so I can study better later.

• *Classic student test answer:* DONKEY HOTEY.

• I used to teach on the college level. Before each test I gave, I spent hours just laughing.

• One quarter I got three F's and one D. That's what I got for studying one subject too much.

• Remember who discovered America: Erik the Leaf.

• Next quarter, I want to arrange my schedule so I don't have any classes.

• Coed overheard in PE class: "I'll stand on my head or bust." The teacher replied, "Just stand on your head."

• *Serious quote from University of Georgia publication:* "Accommodations for 553 married students are provided in University Housing. . . ." My question is: How can you have an odd number of married people?

• *Sign:* **CELERY STALKS AT MIDNIGHT.**

• In college you learn there are actually three sexes—the male sex, the female sex, and insects.

• *Another sign:* Never run away from temptation without leaving a forwarding address.

• Boy, did I learn about art in college! Renoir, Picasso, Cezanne—greatest backfield the Georgia Bulldogs ever had!

• *Boy to boy.* I took Betty out last Saturday night, and do you know what she said? *No?* Oh, you've been out with her too?

intermission

return from intermission

• One night I got sick in college. I headed to the pharmacy, coughing and wheezing, and said to the cashier: "Could you please sell me some cough syrup?"

So the guy casually asked, "Why, do you have a bad cough?"

Pick my answer from this list, considering my brain was racked with fever and I wasn't in the best of mood:

"Do you have a BAD cough?"

A. No, I actually set my hair with cough syrup.
B. Is there any such thing as a GOOD cough?
C. Gimme that bottle, or I'll breathe in your face!

• *Boy to boy.* You got copies of any old Ethics in Journalism tests?

• School? How far did I go? About three blocks.

• Why does the Mona Lisa have that mysterious smile? She knows where to get a decent meal in Athens (name college town).

• *Boy to girl.* May I hold your hand? *Girl:* Of course not. This isn't Palm Sunday! *Boy:* It's not Independence Day either!

• My literary background? I read wallpaper . . . and believe me, it's some trouble turning the pages!

• *Girl:* Were you educated in England? An Oxford man? *Boy:* No, I'm more of the moccasin type.

• At the University I was known as a mental vacuum. That's not usually impressive, but in my class it was.

• Meet professor Schultz, MD, Ph.D, BBS, MAJ. Hmm, that's a strange way to spell Schultz.

• *Roommate:* Close the window! I can't stand the noise of that jet plane! *Second roommate:* That's the Alka-Seltzer you're hearing, Fred.

• *Boy to girl invitation.* There's a lot of weather outside tonight. Ya wanna go look at it?

• Remember, the shortest distance between two points is always near a KEEP OFF THE GRASS sign.

• *Finally, let's take a closer look at some of the University courses which were offered while I was in school. You may want to relate some of these to your college age audiences, just for the educational benefits. By the way, each of these was listed in the University of Georgia Handbook when I was in school. I have added my own course descriptions for your understanding assisted most likely by roommates Tom Beall and Leon Collins.*

ADVANCED GRAMMAR—what Grandpa did.

ADVANCED SHORTHAND—a disease in the advanced stage, caused by hand-to-hand contact, in which the hand slowly becomes shorter.

ART 321—a course which gets down to the bare facts (nudes model in this one).

BASIC IDEAS OF CALCULUS—no such thing.

BEGINNING TYPEWRITING 303—a coursw whuvhteavgrs yor hog tp tupe omt he typwerwtiter.

CERAMICS 260—a down-to-earth crack-pot course.

CRIMINOLOGY—study of how to make money on the side.

FRENCH 103—a course of tongue calisthenics.

HELMINTHOLOGY 803—a study of making crash helmets for motorcyclists and using crash test dummies to prove such.

HISTORICAL GEOLOGY 126—study of Plymouth Rock, Rock of Gilbraltor, Rosetta Stone, etc. (Favorite class expression: "She looked at me like she just stepped on Plymouth Rock and I crawled out from under it.")

INSECTICIDES 477—study of suicides of bugs and their causes.

INTERIOR DESIGN 387—a course designed to keep you out of the cold.

MENTAL HYGIENE 459—a subject everyone needs.

PATHOLOGY 353—the study of ancient trails.

PLANT BREEDING 402—where you learn to tell the sex of a tomato, in case you didn't already know.

POULTRY SCIENCE 360—a foul course.

SHAKESPEARE II—son of William Shakespeare.

SPANISH PHONETICS—a bunch of crazy Spanish people.

SWINE PRODUCTION 476—a study for ham operators.

VISUAL ARTS 317—where you look but don't touch.

WESTERN WORLD LITERATURE 125/126—critical analysis of the life writings of Wyatt Earp, Wild Bill Hickok, Horace Greely, and Kimo Sabby, to mention but a few.

Please do not waste your personal time THANKING ME for sharing this higher learning information. I can feel your gratitude in my psycho even as you read this page. (Yes, I meant to say *psycho.)* Simply delight in the fact that I saved this information for over 20 years just to share it with you. Carry on.

21. Games with Names

MY EARLIER BOOKS *Children Laugh Louder* and *Kidbiz* contained lists of funny names, both real and imaginary, along with ways to add fun using such. A lot has happened in the 13-18 years those books apppeared (and *Children Laugh Louder* is now out-of-print), so between Gene's notebooks, a few other friends, and me, we'll share some new name laughs.

• His name is Basil. He was named after his metabolism.

• Are you ready? Nice to meet you, Ready! *(Sandy Gutherie)*

• Nicole? Do they ever call you nickle? Yes? Do they ever call you five cents? No? Why not? A nickle is five cents! *(Thanks, Roy Porfido!)*

• Things like that made Wyatt Earp.

• He called me aside, but I told him that wasn't my name.

• Your name? John? I've been there.

This little girl has intrigued me the entire time I have worked on the book. A distant relative, her name is Tammy Jo Dent, and the photo was shot in Atlanta @ 1896. I wonder how she talked and walked, who she turned out to be, how her life went. I imagine her sitting on the front row in my audience, enjoying whatever I say or do.

• His name was Will Not. When he was in a hurry, he signed WON'T.

• I'm changing my name to EXIT, so I'll have my name in lights.

• They call him Realtor because he has lots on his mind.

• *John Jacob Jingleheimer Schmidt. His name is my name, too.* Did you ever hear that old camp song? I've always wondered: Is John Jacob Jingleheimer Schmidt the writer's name or my name. Or is my name TOO? Or what? Would somebody please someday explain this to me?

• There are three things I always forget: names, faces, . . . and I forget the other one.

• When I was a kid, we had a white cat named Snowball, a black cat named Midnight, and solid brown dog named Spot. We weren't very creative.

• Actually, we had a cat we called Ben . . . that is, until it had kittens. Then we called it Ben-Hur. *(Thanks to Robert Orben!)*

• What's your name? *(Any answer)* Are you sure? Nice to meet you, Sure! *(Sandy Gutherie)*

• At the party everybody called him Sam. After the party, his wife called him across the carpet.

Steve Taylor of Portland, Oregon, helped play the game with a half dozen lines:

• I found him lying on my doorstep. I called him Matt.

• As a kid I could tread water for hours. People called me Bob.

• Many a girl fell for him. His name was Cliff.

• My friend can only walk on one foot at a time. We call him Skip.

• Do you know the first name of the incredible shrinking man? Les.

• He resembles a lot of his relatives. That's why they named him Gene.

Jeff Dickerson, a wizard with words, sent me a name list to wrap up things here. The moment you hear one of these names, here's a planned ad-lib response:

• PHIL—Shouldn't you be at the bottom of a big hole?

• JACK—Didn't I see you under a car?

• FRANK—Where's ernest? Weren't you in a hot dog bun the other day?

• BILL—I just got one in the mail today!

• BRAD—Could you hold these papers together for me?

• ART—How decorative! Can I hang you on a wall?

• MATT—I saw you at my friend's front door. (I always say, "Oh, Matt, I know your brother, Door." —DG)

- DERRICK—Don't you live in an oilfield?

- NEAL—*An action name. Get on your knees when a kid says that's his name.*

- BARB—You've been sitting on a fence, haven't you?

- DOLLY—Could you help me move some things?

- JOHNNY—Stand here on this spot. Now he's Johnny on the spot!

- CRYSTAL—Clearly a nice name.

- MICKEY—Mouse!

- DWAINE—I have one in my bathtub.

- MIKE—*Action name again. Speak into his head, saying,* "Testing. Testing. One, two, three!"

- PAULA or POLLY—Want a cracker?

- KEN—Okay, where's Barbie?

- Say, are you chewing gum? No, I'm Jeff Dickerson.

22. Money, Money, Money

MONEY INTERESTS everyone in one way or another. Using money is a convenient way of trading, buying, and selling. It makes the world go round, it changes things, it frustrates, it makes happiness, it solves problems, it helps people and hurts them, too.

Money makes some feel important and becomes their identity. Others don't hold it so highly.

Wherever you stand on the money issue, don't let it tell you *who* to be. Be yourself, no matter how little or how much money you possess. And keep your stress level down by seeing the funny in money.

• You've got to say one thing about being poor. It's inexpensive.

• I'm going to join the C.I.O. because everyone I see—I owe.

• He was so tight with money, when he took a dollar from his pocket, George Washington blinked at the light.

• I was in the Everything's A Dollar store the other day, and the cashier called out over the loud speaker, "Price check!" *(Bruce Johnson)*

• *Another:* He used to work in the Everything's A Dollar store, but he couldn't remember the prices.

• For my allowance I used to get ten cents a week, but dimes have changed.

• I had some money left me. Yes, it left me.

• We are so used to putting coins in a slot to get things, we sort of expect the Lord to give us something for each coin we drop in the collection plate.

• Money is the best substitute there is for credit.

• I just saw a big billboard saying "BUY AMERICAN!" and in the corner of the sign it says, "Made in Japan!"

• It's all in the way you look at things. Two men were working on a construction site. When asked what they were doing, one replied, "I'm working for $12 an hour." The other replied, "I'm building a cathedral."

• Price ceiling—when I heard the price, I hit the ceiling.

• Save your money. It may be valuable some day.

• Men get their pictures on money. Women get their hands on it.

• When I was a kid, my family was so poor we couldn't pay attention.

• My salary? I get ten percent of the gate for all people over ninety if accompanied by their parents.

• My father used to give me a weekly allowance of a dollar and a pat on the head. By the time I was 14, I had $350 and a flat head.

• In England, they used to deal with shillings and pence. There was a big difference in shillings and pence. For instance, you could walk down the street without any shillings, but you couldn't walk down the street without any pence.

• He was so poor, the mice in his house got a care package from the mice across the street.

• This money is educated. Every cent counts!

• I know where you can get a T-bone for one dollar. If you want a steak with it, that's $12 more.

• A dime is a dollar with the taxes taken out.

• Thank you for the bill. I'll pay you back when I get my Social Security check. You see, I'm a bill collector.

• I bought this item with my credit card. It came from Paris, France. It was made here in the USA and sold to a wholesaler. The wholesaler sold it to a retailer in Paris, and that's the guy who sold it to me. Just think of all those people who are making a living out of something I haven't even paid for yet!

• Inflation used to creep up on us. Now it stands up and walks.

• What good is happiness? It can't buy money.

• Do you know a sure-fire way to become a millionaire? It's easy. Just go to the bank every week and deposit $20,000. At the end of the year, you're a millionaire.

• The younger generation will learn the value of money when they begin paying off our debts.

• Save your pennies, and the sales tax will take care of them.

• There once was a time when a fool and his money were soon parted, but now it happens to everybody.

• A penny saved is a penny you didn't report to the IRS.

• I've got the first dollar I ever made. You know, there aren't many of those Confederate bills still around.

• I always have too much month at the end of my money.

• Thank you for the donation which will go to my favorite charity—an orphan's home of which I am President, Secretary and Treasurer. I am also the orphan.

• I borrowed $2,000 from my uncle so I could study law. My first case was when my Uncle sued me for $2,000.

• A dollar may not go as far as it used to, but what it lacks in distance, it makes up for in speed.

• I only do this show to earn money because I have an expensive hobby. I like to eat.

Funny Money Facts

• It costs 4.1 cents to print a $1 bill, same for a $100 bill.

• In circulation, coins last 15 years average. A $1 bill lasts 18 months, a $20 bill lasts 4 years, $50 and $100 bills last 9 years.

• The largest U.S. bill ever put into circulation was the $10,000 bill with Salmon P. Chase on its face.

• It costs .6 cent to make a U.S. penny. In other words, about 2/3 of a penny to make a penny!

• You can fold a dollar bill back and forth about 4000 times before it will tear. It's strong!

• Which U.S. President is on the $100 bill? (See p. 171)

• If you had ten billion $1 bills and spent one every second of every day, it would take you 317 years to spend all that cash!

23. Magicians by Trade

WE'RE A FUNNY BREED, magicians, in more ways than one. But when we make fun of ourselves, we're simply proving we're as human as anyone else. It's just that we can do some things that other people cannot do.
We all have gifts and talents, plus we all have traits somebody can pick on. Why not create fun by picking on ourselves?

• I can just see that you people are thinking, "He doesn't look like a magician." Lots of magicians wear a moustache and a goatee, and they try to make you think they look like the devil. Well, most of them do!

• I said, "Could you hire a magician like me?" And he said, "Yes, if he isn't too much like you."

• This was invented by a Hindu magician over three hundred years ago. He gave it to me himself.

• In olden times magicians were burned at the stake or had their heads chopped off. But they always had their choice—chop or steak.

• We magicians used to make people disappear into thin air. Now there's no longer any thin air.

• My first job in magic was with a one-ring circus in Kentucky. I used to fill in while the elephants changed clothes. I didn't want to play second fiddle

David Ginn, age 7, in the tube, with neighbor friend Lynn Shimp standing. Lynn showed me my first three magic tricks and even gave them to me years later, starting me on this career of trickery and fun.

to elephants, but I couldn't help it. They carried more weight. The boss liked them because they worked for peanuts . . . and they carried their own trunks.

• I would rather starve than do anything else but magic. Now I do both.

• Some people ask, "How do you become a magician?" Well, you wander into a magic shop some day and buy a couple of tricks. Then you fool your friends, buy some more tricks, and you become the life of the party. Then some people say, "You ought to go on the stage." Like an idiot, you believe them.

• A magician is a man who can find a seat on a rush-hour bus. In other words, a magician can do the impossible. I think you will agree after seeing this show, that I, too, am impossible.

• My ability as a magician is only exceeded by my courage.

• Performing magic is for people who have never had a nervous breakdown but always wanted one.

• A world without magic would be a world that has lost its sense of surprise. Besides, it's fun to be fooled for a change by someone who is *supposed* to fool you.

• I'm a self-made magician. I started at the bottom, and I liked it so well that I stayed there.

• Does your mother know that you are a miracle worker? Or would she say it's a miracle when you work?

• I sawed women in half when I was a child magician. Why, I have three half sisters to prove it.

• How do we magicians perform our feats? Of course, it's all very simple, if you are born that way.

• I'm so sentimental, I cry at card tricks.

• What made me a magician? It's because I was the ninth child in a family of eight.

• *Show the audience a picture of yourself.* "Here's a picture of me with Houdini." Someone will say, "You're the only one in the picture," or "That's just you." Look at the picture quizically. "Well, whatta you know—*Houdini escaped again!*"

24. Magic Props

REAL PEOPLE are not accustomed to seeing magicians' painted boxes, tubes, scarves, and other paraphernalia. Some of the objects look very strange and mysterious to non-magicians.

To lighten up the mystery, and in an attempt to normalize or at least explain that object of wonder, try some of these lines. Make 'em more fun.

• There are many people who probably have no idea what this is for—and I am one of those people.

• Would you swoon with delight if I let you examine this? I know it's thrilling, but try to stand the excitement a little longer.

My first top hat, only I can't find it! David at six months.

• I call these shears Julius because that was scissor's first name.

• This used to be part of a hope chest—but it turned out hopeless.

• If you think you lead a hard life, think of the blows this handkerchief receives.

• We've had this plate ever since it was a saucer.

• If anyone desires to examine this apparatus—I would appreciate it if you would just stay in your seat and mind your own business.

• Everyone recognizes this as an ordinary, everyday *quark*. As we all know, a quark is an elementary entity of matter consisting of positive and negative parts moving in all directions with the velocity of light, capable of passing through solids, according to the theory of Lansmuir. But tonight I shall use it merely to cover this tumbler.

• What's an antique? It's a piece of junk that costs a lot!

• This hammer used to belong to George Washington. Of course, since then it has had two new heads and four new handles. *Adapt to other common objects.*

• This is an antique. It goes back to Louis XIV. I have a TV set that goes back to Sears on the 15th. *(Very old, but still funny.)*

• I use this as a wand. It's an object that was first seen many centuries ago under the seventh moon of the Ramadon, during the reign of the Antiphigistines in the Haletosis period. Put it under your pillow, and it gives peace to those who sleep at night.

• This was invented by an old sea captain. On his deathbed, he told his two sons that he wanted to be buried at sea. The sad part is—both sons were drowned trying to dig his grave.

• Playing cards came over to America with Columbus, but the sailors couldn't play cards because Columbus sat on the deck.

• This is made of mad steel. It's lost its temper.

• This water makes me think of the time I nearly drowned. I was lying there in my bed—the pillow slipped, the bed spread, and I fell into the springs.

• This card trick reminds me of the Great Poker Mystery—when the stovepipe fell, soot followed soot.

• They used this for a cage at one time for that rare bird called the MOA. It's extinct now—there is no MOA.

• This prop used to belong to King Antiphigistine. You've probably heard of him if you ever studied monotony.

• I used to do this trick with Steamboat cards, but I fell through the deck. I used Bee cards, but I got stung. Next I tried Bicycle cards, but I was always tired. Finally, I tried Congress cards, but they were always on vacation.

The Great DeFoliette, traveling magician, @ 1927, in his attempt at the Vanishing Car trick. Instead, the leaves fell off the nearby trees. Actually, it's my wife's Uncle Lee Smith standing by the convertible with his friend Slim "out catching air"somewhere in Texas.

25. Mistakes We Make

TWELVE YEARS AGO, the day three-year-old Todd climbed the kitchen counter and pulled the chocolate layer cake—the cake his mom Cindy had spent all afternoon making—onto the floor, my first thought was to punish him severely. But he wasn't my child.

By the time Cindy called my house and told me about the incident, she was laughing.

"Just as well to laugh as to cry," she told me, "because crying won't change things."

Maybe she was right. We all make mistakes. Accidents do happen. Our job as performers is to make the best of circumstances and keep the show rolling. After all, we learn from mistakes and accidents more than if things went right all the time.

From the moment they placed him atop the mule, young Robert knew he had made a big mistake. Or they had! Lithonia, Georgia, @ 1925. An unhappy boy.

"Good judgment comes from experience," a saying goes, "and experience comes from bad judgment." Mistakes, accidents, poor judgments. Tackle them, solve them, live through them. They're only temporary. Laugh at them, too. You'll grow.

• I may not be good, but at least I'm different.

• In fact, I am what is known as the Disaster of Ceremonies.

• This looks like a cross between perhaps and *mishaps*.

• I'll finish this thing if it kills you.

• As Heinz would say, "There are 57 ways of doing it!"

• What can you expect with a day that begins by getting up in the morning?

• How do you like that? I've never done it that way!

• If I'd tried to make that funny, it wouldn't have been. Now, why IS that?

• Did you hear the one about the magician who tried stupid tricks that didn't work?

• Hmph! Magic! Comedy! It's a tough job—but somebody has to do it!

• Oooh! I feel groaning pains!

• When something goes wrong, pull an index card out of your pocket and toss it aside, saying, "I'll never use that one again!"

• That's strange. It worked when David Copperfield did it!

• Remember, folks: Now YOU have a friend in the goof-it-up business.

@ 1920. Big mistake. My grandfather's brother, Leonard "Len" Ginn, let them know it was his birthday, so he got a "friendly" whipping. Years later I married a girl named Lynne to make her another Lynne Ginn.

• Ever since I was a boy, I have wanted to do this in the worst way—and now I am doing it in the worst way!

• Oh, well, perfection can be boring.

• I did it that way just to make sure it wouldn't work. I was right.

• Confucius said, "Knowledge is boundless, but the capacity of one man is limited." I think what I just did proves Confucius was absolutely right.

• I really don't know how that happened. I never make mistakes. Why, one time I *thought* I made a mistake—but I was wrong.

26. Music and Musicians

COMEDY AND MUSIC often go hand in hand to compliment each other. Music played poorly can cause laughter, and so can music played well, if humor is your aim.

Chuck Berry said it—"Roll over, Beethoven, tell Tchaikovsky the news." Whether it's big band, disco, rap, country, or good old rock-n-roll, let's laugh about it.

• This orchestra is just like one big family. They go out together, sleep together, eat together—some day they'll learn to play together.

• The trombone player was fired for indulging in subversive activities—someone caught him taking music lessons.

• Play that tune that's a descriptive number from the fifth movement of the third man in conga time.

It's a melody about a Cherokee hitchhiker called "Indian Thumbee."

• I see that song did something to you. It made you sick.

• I've heard you sing, and I think you should have your tonsils out. Oh, you've had them out? Then put them back in.

• You've never played the piano better. Kind of sad when you come to think of it.

• Look what you've done to my song.

• Imitation of Pavoratti *(stand still, do nothing)*— waiting between two songs.

Strike up the band! My grandfather, Fred H. Ginn, played guitar (back right) in this 1900 group.

• Do I play the piano? Well, what else can I do with it?

• I sang in a church choir and four hundred people changed their religion.

• I'll do the elevator dance. See—no steps.

• Do you know how to save a piano player from drowning? I'm glad to hear that you do.

• This orchestra is one of the finest aggravations in the country.

• He's an excellent musician and a fine fellow to boot.

Later Fred Ginn played cornet in the Lithonia Silver Band. He's the 2nd horn from the left.

• What? Me—sing? Why, I've got a voice that even an echo won't answer.

• Why don't you clean the piano? Half the keys are black.

• His voice is changing from terrible to horrible.

• She says she's a piano teacher, but that's silly. What can you teach a piano?

• With his brother's help, he used to have a singing trio. His brother had two heads.

• His fingers are so fast on that keyboard, he can play Chopin's Minute Waltz in 18 seconds.

• He used to play the harp, but churches made him stop. He discouraged too many people from going to heaven.

• Play me some sad music. *Pause.* I said sad, not pitiful.

Steve Taylor shared the next four:

• I sometimes can sing High C, but I can always sing LOUSY.

• When I sing people clap—their hands over their ears.

• I once won second place in a singing contest. Of course, there were only two contestants. I sang first, and once the judges heard me sing, they gave the other guy first place.

• When I sing, some people say my voice is cultivated. Most say it should be plowed under!

• Rock-and-roll may be here to stay, but it will never take the place of the old-fashioned earache.

• I knew he had music in his soul—I heard his shoes squeak.

27. Television

WHEN LYNNE AND I were first married, Abb Dickson stopped by our apartment one day. We had inherited an old black and white TV set that formerly belonged to my grandparents. It had a funny hexagonal-shaped picture screen.

Abb looked at that thing and asked, "Does it show *only* old movies?"

We've never forgotten that.

Growing up in the television age, we've seen the good and bad sides of TV. We've seen the medium abused, and we've watched it put to good use.

If you are in a position to improve the wonder-filled medium of television, by all means do that. If not, the least you can do is make fun of it!

• People ask me why I don't try to do this act on television. Little do they know, I'm still trying to get it on radio.

• It was one of those suspense movies. It kept me wondering— "What's on TV?"

• I can tell you are a TV fan—you have square eyeballs.

• When I was a kid, we had only three channels, and it was always hard to decide what to watch. Nowadays, there's 150 channels . . . and NOTHING to watch! *(Steve Taylor)*

• I won this on a TV quiz show. I didn't know the truth, and this was the consequence.

• I went on a quiz show and won a trip to Bermuda. There was only one catch to it—I had to shovel coal both ways.

• With all those commercials on television, you feel so silly punishing a child for lying.

• And TV commercials really open a lot of doors— the refrigerator door, the bathroom door, the closet door.

• Remember the good old days when baseball players shaved at home instead of on television.

• When I was a boy, children were out on the streets, constantly exposed to criminals, violence, and corruption. Thanks to TV, today they can be exposed to all that in the privacy of their own homes.

• I saw a great stag movie last night. It was called *Bambi*.

• This year the main idea on television seems to be providing, as cheaply and easily as possible, something to fill the time between commercials.

• Speaking for myself and reflecting the opinion of many others, let me say that it is a poisonous experience to look at yourself on a television screen and listen to the sound of your own voice. You lose all faith in humanity.

28. Husbands and Wives

ONCE THERE was a jigsaw puzzle with only two pieces. Each piece thought it was more important, but without both pieces interlocked there was no completed picture. Finally, both parts realized that *without mutual cooperation,* nothing worked. The name of this puzzle was marriage.

• Always be kind to your wife. I certainly am. I always hold the door open for mine when she starts on her paper route.

• Ladies, you must remember that marriage consists of give and take. If he doesn't give enough, just take it!

• I've got my wife trained the right way. She gets her own breakfast.

• Our dog is adopted. My wife and I couldn't have one.

• It takes two to make a marriage—a girl and her mother.

My grandparents, Ida Grey and Fred Ginn, married in 1913, without whom there would be no Frank Ginn and no David Ginn.

• I've got to go now. If I'm not home in a couple of hours, my wife rents out my room.

• He comes from a mixed marriage. His father was a man, and his mother was a woman.

• *Woman's hair, beautiful hair*
What words of praise I utter.
But oh, how sick it makes me feel
To find it in the butter.

• If your wife wants a pearl necklace, get her a bushel of oysters and wish her luck.

• He thought he married a rich widow. Then he found out she had buried her husband in a rented

My other grandparents, Edwin and Hassie Mae Matthews, married in 1908, who had five children, including my mother, Helen.

tuxedo and lost all her money keeping up the payments.

• We've never gone to bed mad. Of course, one year we were up for three months.

• Momma Bear to Papa Bear: "This is absolutely my last year as den mother!"

• Marriage is a gamble that often wins a full house.

• I just discovered that the dictionary was written when Noah Webster had a fight with his wife. One word led to another.

• I know a fellow in Minnesota who went ice fishing. He brought home 200 pounds of ice. His wife fried it, the ice melted, and they both drowned.

• My wife claims I snore, but I've never heard such a thing.

• Her father put a silencer on his shotgun, since his daughter wanted a quiet wedding.

• Marriage is like a midnight phone call. You get a ring, then you wake up.

• His wife makes the best meals you ever thaw.

• What a husband! He absolutely loves work. He could sit on the porch and watch his wife garden for hours.

• He was a human fly. One day he got into an argument with his wife, and she swatted him.

• Adam and Eve had an ideal marriage. He didn't hear about men she could have married, and she didn't hear about the way his mother cooked.

• He has been married to her for thirty years. Blames it on a Lonely Hearts Club that lied in their advertising—it said ten days free trial.

• I was going to take my wife on a vacation to the Thousand Islands and spend a day on each, but I that would take too long.

• It is better to have loved a short man than not to have loved a tall.

29. Audience Helpers

GENERALLY, PEOPLE in the audience of any show love to come on stage. TV quiz shows are a fine example of this, as are the performances of magicians from David Copperfield to birthday party magicians and clowns.

And even though only a few persons actually help onstage, they vicariously "stand in" for everyone else in the crowd who would like to be in their shoes. That's why it is so important for performers to select helpers from all over the audience, not just the front row.

Here are some words and ways to entice helpers onto your stage, joke with them while they are there, and send them away feeling good.

• Will you come up? Yes, you—at least it looks like you.

• I shall be glad to have the assistance of a gentleman from the audience, preferably one who has never seen me before or if not, one who wishes never to see me again.

• This is your chance to come up. Today is short, yesterday is gone, tomorrow may never come, so don't be backward about coming forward.

• Did you twist your tongue around your eye-teeth so you couldn't see what you're doing?

• Wait a moment. Are you sure that you thoroughly misunderstand me?

• Some day I want you to come over to my house and play in my poison ivy garden.

• Relax. You're as nervous as a turkey in November.

• Could I have a lock of your hair? I'm stuffing a mattress. Hey, I'm letting you off easy. I was going to ask for the whole wig!

• Oh, you're a Navy man, a sailor. Sailors speak in maritime terms. They use knots instead of miles because they want the ocean tied.

• Turn around and face the music like a man.

• Would you like to be a good magician? I know I would!

• Come right onto the stage and bring both feet with you.

• I would have enjoyed having you go hunting with me—I had my other two hounds along.

• It makes me very happy that you came all this way just to visit me.

• What's your name? Bill? Now the questions get tougher as we go along.

• Don't worry. But if you must worry, worry somebody else, not me.

• Would you like to make a wish? What? You wish you hadn't come up here?

• *As child holds prop to open.* If you have given up trying to open something, tell a four-year-old not to touch it!

• What's your name? *(Wait for answer.)* Well, you couldn't help that.

• What you have just said has brought new meaning to the word *trivia*.

• It's wonderful for me to be here with you, and I hope you appreciate it.

• Come up, please. You can see better up here.

• *Troublesome helper.* After the show, could I drop you off somewhere? Say, the Grand Island Bridge?

• Come up, come up. Move the feet and the body will follow.

• I need someone to time this trick. Does someone have a watch with a second hand? You have one—yes, I can see it's second hand.

• Excuse me. I've forgotten your first name, and I can't remember your last.

• I would like to have a stranger help me. Would you? You look a little strange to me.

• *Giggling helper.* Have you been taking those funny pills again?

• Just when did you fall out of the hearse?

• Count up to five. See if you can do it from memory.

• Sir, you are annoying the man I love. *(Meaning yourself, you the performer.)*

• Have you ever seen me before? Well, aren't you glad!

• Goodbye, Mary Ruth *(girl's name)*. Partying is such sweet sorry—I mean PARTING is such sweet sorrow. Remember, as you go through life, we once stood in the spotlight and had our one moment in time. Yes, it was wonderful, blissful, heart-warming—and it killed five minutes!

• Smile big—it adds to your face value.

• What did you say your name was? Good, I wanted to know if you still remembered it.

• How old are you? What? Thirty-three? Why, you don't look a day over 40!

• Now, sir, will you point to a strange lady? Will you come up here, strange lady?

Strange lady? Perhaps not in the year 1910. I don't know who she is—some relative—but she seems to be thoughtfully considering the merit of something I have just said or done in my performance. She also seems ready to whack me over the head with that paper in her hand!

- Isn't this wonderful? You two just arrived onstage, and already the audience is giving you a sitting ovation.

- *To lady helper.* Were you ever a Girl Scout? No? What a coincidence. I never was either.

- Would you kindly take a seat in this chair. The doctor will be with you in a minute.

- *To helper much younger than you.* I hope I look as well as you do when I get to be your age.

- You're a good egg, George. Once in a while I find one that's cracked.

- *To fancy-dressed lady or man.* Thanks for dressing up for my show. I really appreciate it.

- Do you believe in the hereafter? Well, hereafter you will!

- You can always tell your left hand. It's always on the same side as your left foot.

- You look like a kind person. I'll soon find out what kind.

- *To helper yawning:* What time would you like to be called in the morning?

- *To pretty girl:* Tell me about yourself—your troubles, your dreams, your hopes, your telephone number.

- Have you ever met me before? Well, have you ever met me after?

- *Sawing a girl in half:* Are you married or single? It doesn't really matter. In a minute you'll be separated.

- She's just my type—a girl!

- What do you do for a living? Oh, you eat!

30. Christmas

ROBERT ORBEN once wrote, "Christmas is the time of year when people stay up until three in the morning playing 'Silent Night' on the radio." I like the humor in that. It speaks to me of the incongruity of people's actions at that time of year.

"Peace on Earth, but buy the Killer Komando Power toy!" might be another side of the story. Not the real story of Christ's birth, but the story of our commercialized world.

I love Christmas for many reasons. First, for the Baby in the manger—God's great gift to mankind. Second, for the good feelings people usually have for their fellow man during that season of the year. Third, for the smiling faces of children expecting a magic visit from Santa.

Fourth, for the opportunity to say "I love you" and "thank you" to family, friends, and co-workers—sharing a gift, a card, a handshake, or a hug.

This Christmas, please joke with joy.

- Christmas—it's that time of year when you drag a dead tree into the house and eat candy out of a sock!

• Last Christmas I finally gave her a fur piece—a Davy Crockett coonskin cap. It made her look good in a way . . . far away!

December 25, 1922. Frank Ginn, age 20 months, socks falling down, his drawers (underware) hanging out, discovers a train under the tree!

- Ah, Christmas! I can hear carolers singing those timeless words, "Children roasting on an open fire!"

- Remember the words from "The Night Before Christmas?" These: "The stockings were hung by the chimney with care, and believe me the room could use some *fresh air!*" Oh, and there's more: "And I heard him exclaim as he flew out of sight— 'Quick! Land the sleigh! My seatbelt's too tight!'"

- Christmas is the time of year where you go into debt in the future to pay for the present.

- For Christmas this year, I sent my dad a check for $100. Now if he'd only sign it, and mail it back to me!

- Riddle: Why did Santa plant three rows of beans in his garden? Because he wanted to HOE, HOE, HOE! *(Oh, oh, oh!)*

- What nationality is Santa Claus? Why, he's North Polish!

- A little boy came home from Sunday School and told his mom, "The name of the King of Israel is BORN." "How do you know that?" asked the mother. And the little guy replied, "Because we sang, 'BORN is the King of Israel!'"

- I'd get some Christmas seals, but what do you feed them?

- Christmas always begins with one question: WHERE do you pay TOO MUCH for HOW MANY of WHICH KIND of WHATEVER IT IS to give to WHOM?

David Ginn (age 7) and sister Nancy (age 4) visiting that "jolly old elf" himself in the magical 1950s! Merry Christmas!

• It's the time of year we men receive a tie that's in a clash by itself.

• Let's sing my favorite Christmas song: "When shepherds washed their socks by night."

• On Christmas day, it's the mother who separates the toys from the men.

• If you have a dog, he probaby enjoys the Christmas tree. Only time of the year he has indoor plumbing.

• Five minutes after the gifts are ripped open, Christmas is over!

• "Jingle Bells, shotgun shells, Santa's gone astray—"

• At this time of year, you can make people forget the past with a present.

• I was in the bank and wanted to join the Christmas Club, but I don't have time to attend meetings.

• Look into a child's eyes, listen to a child's laughter, and be humbly grateful that you are privileged to live in a world where Christmas lives.

• I love Christmas. It's the time of year when Santa comes down the chimney and savings go down the drain!

• Look into a child's eyes and see there the tremendous eternal miracle of Christmas. Discover there what has made Christmas live when a thousand other customs have been trampled under the feet of the passing years.

Answer to page 142:

Benjamin Franklin is pictured on the U.S. one dollar bill, but this is a trick question. He was never President of the United States of America!

Seriously, how many of you have a photograph of your great-grandmother holding you as a baby? Well, I do!

Here is Ada Pratt, my grandmother Ida Grey's mother, sitting on the back of a car in 1946 holding me, baby David. That's small town for you—East Atlanta, which was a small town-like little community at the time. Church, school, grocery store, and movie theatre were only two blocks away!

31. Small Town

A HUNDRED YEARS ago comedians were picking on small towns. They'll still do it 100 years from now. Yet even though we poke fun at small town life, conditions, and habits, most of us realize that those places are the heart of real family values.

My wife Lynne grew up in Sylvester, Georgia, about 200 miles south of Atlanta. The city population was 4000, with about 8000 total in the county. Everybody knew everybody else or knew about them. There weren't too many secrets.

On the other hand, I grew up in Atlanta, a big city to Lynne—but with a difference: my little community of East Atlanta was like a small town. One main street had all the stores—florist, grocery, bakery, pharmacy, barber shop, appliance store, movie theatre, fire station, hamburger joint, restaurant, 5 and 10 store . . . and the elementary school was around the corner.

For eight years I walked two blocks to school, K-7 grade. I walked to the movie show, acted as a school safety patrol, went to church, attended Boy Scouts, had picnics in the park, performed my earliest magic shows—all within a four-block area of my home. It was small town, and I had a wonderful childhood there, thanks to my parents and grandparents and friends. Thanks to magic, too.

Even those who have moved away still have small town in their hearts. Most of us secretly long to be back there, or a place much like that, where life was simpler than it is today.

Enough nostalgia. What is the flavor of a small town? I think . . . vanilla.

• A small town is a place where everyone knows whose check is good and whose husband isn't. — *Lynne Miller Ginn*

• That town was so small the power plant was a Die Hard battery.

• The tour bus never leaves the station.

• A small town is a place where it's no sooner done than said.

• I sent a description of myself to Sears Roebuck, and they photographed me by mail.

• It may be small, but it's a good town. I'd live there myself if I knew the language.

• When I shave there with my electric razor, the main street lights dim.

• You're from Batavia, New York? *(Adapt locally.)* That's quite a place. Our church sent a missionary there once.

• Our town was so small we didn't even have a village idiot, so we all took turns.

• There are only three things of interest in Smallville: that's morning, noon, and night. If some fellow appears on the street wearing a white collar any day other than Sunday, immediately a crowd gathers. It's so healthy there, they had to shoot two men to start a cemetary.

• I like this town. I'm coming back when it's completed.

• My hometown was so small, the zip code was a decimal point. The four-way stop only goes two ways.

Okay. I had chickens in my own backyard growing up in East Atlanta, and so did my wife's family in South Georgia.

Proof: Here is Lynne's own brother, Frankie Miller, amusing himself as a child by playing with a dead chicken, around 1946, in the town of Arlington, Georgia, waiting on Sunday dinner.

What Frankie did not realize is—he was playing with the main course!

• I have two brothers—one living and one in Mechanicsburg, PA. *(Adapt.)*

• In our town the steeple clock had four faces, and each told a different time. It made no difference, though. Nobody went anywhere.

• I came from a small town where there was nothing doing every minute.

• I wasn't born here, but I'm sure dying here.

• My hometown was so small that if you put a four-way cold tablet in the center of town, it wouldn't have any place to go. If the tide went out, it never would come back in.

32. Work

I DON'T KNOW how I learned to work, but it's always made sense to me. My personal frustration is that I don't have enough *time* to do everything I want to do—writing, performing, traveling, lecturing, doing projects like videos. I enjoy work because it is *fun work*, and basically it helps people and makes them happy. And that's a reward better than money.

• A very disturbing thing happened in Detroit the other day, where the world's first fully automated factory is in operation. Six of the machines got together and asked for an oil break.

• I just planted three trees, and I used elephant fertilizer. I want them to have big trunks.

• I'm going to be like Robinson Crusoe and have all my work done by Friday.

• The only trouble with doing nothing is that you can't stop and rest. Furthermore, you never know when you're finished. *(Robert Orben, first part; Steve Taylor, second.)*

• We were really busy today. The computer broke down, and we all had to think.

• The people who complain the loudest about capital and labor are usually the ones who never had any capital and never did any labor.

• I didn't go to that dry cleaner's place. His sign read "Fifteen Years on the Same Spot." I didn't have that long to wait.

• If all the unemployed people suddenly went to work, all the people working in the unemployment bureaus would be unemployed.

• He used to work in a winery, stepping on grapes. He got fired when he was caught sitting down on the job.

• I used to be a novelty worker. It was a novelty when I worked.

• It's easier today than ever before to make an honest living. There's so little competition.

Work in the 1930's. Henry Smith, my wife's mother's brother, working for Standard Oil Company delivering gasoline.

- Automation has opened up for skilled employees a whole new world of unemployment.

- He worked for peanuts until he proved his salt. Now he gets salted peanuts.

- Well, this is better than working. I used to do imaginative work. I used to imagine what work was like.

- Is that fellow a salesman? You bet he is! Why, he sold two milking machines to a farmer who had only one cow, then he took the cow for down payment!

- Things won't change much in the completely automated office or factory. The button that gets ahead will still be the one with the most push.

• My boss offered me an interest in the business. At least that's what I thought. He said if I didn't take an interest soon, he'd fire me.

• I succeeded by exercising long hours of hard work and a total disregard for quality.

• His insomnia has gotten so bad that he can't even sleep at work.

• I'm working for a good cause. ME—'cause I need the money!

33. Parenting

WITH CHILDREN, life is just one thing after another, an adventure to be sure. People thought I knew a lot about kids before I had my own child because I entertained them so well in shows. But the truth is that I have learned infinitely more about kids in the last seventeen years with a child growing up in my house.

Through sickness and health, good and bad times, successes and failures, Lynne and I have become official parents. But it's not over. Someone recently told me, "When your kids go off to college or get married, your parenting job is only half done." Previews of coming attractions!

• Insanity can be contagious. You can get it from your children.

• A boy is an appetite with skin pulled over it.

- You know what they say, boys will be noise.

- Have your children young. Who wants old children?

- In the old days, a juvenile delinquent was a boy with an overdue library book.

- As a parent, your best ability is *availability*.

- The best time for parents is when the kids are too old to cry and too young to borrow the car.

- My mother was mad about children. She'd have given anything if I'd have been one.

- When I was born, I was so surprised—I couldn't talk for a year and a half.

- After the wedding, you haven't lost a daughter—you've gained a bathroom.

- I recently read a magazine article penned by a well-known writer, and I thought you might like to hear part of it. This author was deeply disturbed by the juvenille delinquency in his community, which prompted his writing of these stinging comments:
"Our youth love luxury. They have bad manners, contempt for authority, and disrespect for older people. Even the younger people are tyrants. They no longer rise when their elders enter the room. They contradict their parents, talk before company, gobble their food, and disobey their teachers."
Maybe you kids are not so bad, since these words were written in the 5th Century B.C.—464 years before Christ. The writer's name was Socrates.

• Although your children are deductible, they can also be very taxing.

• If a child is spoiled, it's probably because you can't spank two grandmothers.

Fred and Ida Grey Ginn with baby James Franklin Ginn, in 1922. Professional backdrop: a bedsheet hung on a clothesline!

• Parents are always being blamed for juvenile delinquency, but I don't know. Chickens come from broken homes, and they turn out all right . . . especially on a rotisserie.

• You don't have to worry about confused teenagers. Just give them time, and they'll grow up to be confused adults.

• Just like all the boys of his age, he's concerned about ecology. He said, "We have to do something about cleaning up the environment." His father said, "That's great! You can start with your room." You should see the boy's room—he won't let anyone touch it. He said, "Leave it alone. I know where everything is." And he does—on the floor! One time his mother brought in a vacuum cleaner and it threw up!

• Who raised this younger generation that we're criticizing so much?

• Some of these kids seem as if their parents embarked on the sea of matrimony without a paddle.

• A babysitter is a teenager who behaves like an adult when the adults are out behaving like teenagers.

• The trouble with some of today's smart kids is that they don't smart in the right place.

• I love babies. They brighten up the home. We have the lights on all night.

• No two children are alike, particularly if one is yours and the other one isn't.

• She knitted three socks for her son because he wrote her that he had grown another foot in the army.

• Last night I slept like a baby. I woke up crying every two hours.

• A little boy never said a word for the first six years of his life. One day his parents served him spaghetti, and the kid spoke up, saying, "This spaghetti is no good!" His parents jumped up and shouted, "Why did you wait so long to talk?" He said, "Up till now, everything's been okay."

• Before I go, I have a message for all you parents. Sometime when your teenage son or daughter is out for the evening, take advantage of the opportunity. Pack up your furniture, call a moving van, and don't leave a forwarding address!

• If only I could be confident that my kids were sleeping—and not recharging!

• My parents moved three times before I was five, but I found them every time!

• He started out to be a child delinquent. Both parents neglected him. They were so busy neither of them were home when he was born.

• His parents were gypsies, and when he was four years old, he was kidnapped by a band of bankers.

• A lot of people can trace their families back three hundred years, but they don't know where their kids are at night.

SCHOOL CHILDREN GET THEATER PARTY
Jerrie Kramer, Sue Breedlove Are 2 of 6,000

Early 1950s. I had read my ten library books, and along with 6000 other kids I went to Atlanta's Fox Theatre for the free movie. Just as the photographer shot, dad Frank Ginn boosted me up, and we made the Sunday Atlanta Journal & Constitution.

• He's strange. He was born an only twin.

• I don't know what I would have done if there were teenagers when I was young.

• How did I handle my youth? I bored my parents doing magic tricks all day long. When I was nine years old, they ran away from home!

• That crook was so dumb he kidnapped a boy once and sent him home with the ransom note. Then the kid's folks sent the boy back with the money.

• Some kids are like thermometers. They are graduated, have degrees, then hang around the house.

• Remember, parents, they're all angels when they are asleep. —*David Ginn*

34. Weather

IN MARCH 1993, Lynne, Autumn, and I traveled to Oslo, Norway, for a magic convention. Afterwards we took the train to Bergen, a ten-hour mountain ride through a snowy, winter wonderland. In Bergen the next day we experienced rain, sleet, snow, sunshine, plus more rain and snow the same day. Now *that* was weather to talk about!

Seems like everyone talks about the weather. According to Skip Light, in Illinois there are only two seasons: winter and construction.

In Hawaii the weather is so nice that flowers bloom every day of the year. In Antarctica, the two seasons are frozen and thawed. And if the local weather man predicts rain, look outside your window before you believe it.

Personally, I keep an umbrella in my car at all times. You never know who to trust.

• Hot weather doesn't bother me. I just throw the thermometer out the window and watch the temperature drop.

• *Perspiring performer.* Hey—I'm defrosting!

• It's so cold the politicians have their hands in their own pockets.

• How do you know when it's springtime in Athens? *(Name a city near a river.)* The garbage in the Oconee River turns GREEN! *(Thanks, Abb Dickson.)*

• Isn't this wonderful weather? Every morning you can open the window and listen to the birds coughing.

• Buffalo is going to deal with pollution as soon as it can see its way clear. *(Substitute the closest large city to you.)*

• Nice thing about rain—you don't have to shovel it.

• It's so cold here that the natives go to Siberia in the winter.

• No one writes fiction as well as the weather forecaster.

• Snow can cause a heart attack. Just ask any kid what he charges to shovel your driveway!

Before we leave the subject of weather, let's take a quick look at the two extremes . . . and offer over a dozen quips for the temperatures.

How Cold Was It?
Man, it was SO COLD that—

• Snakes crawled south for the winter.

• My telephone line froze up.

• When I blew out my breath, it spelled—GET ME INSIDE!

• We now have only 49 states. New Hampshire and Vermont froze together.

• The traffic light outside has changed from red to blue.

• I saw a dog wearing a cat! *(Roy Porfido)*

• When my freezer broke down, nothing thawed out.

• Speaking of cold, now I know what "The Big Chill" really means!

• It's so cold—if I smile, my face may crack!

How Hot Was It?
Man, it was SO HOT—

• My ice cream cone is now a milkshake!

• My air conditioner needs an air conditioner!

• My deodorant melted!

• The cows gave evaporated milk!

• My rabbit took off his fur coat.

• I had to feed the chickens crushed ice to keep them from laying hard-boiled eggs!

Not too hot, not too cold. My dad's first cousin, Vera Plunkett, at age five, playing on their grandparents front porch in Lithonia, Georgia, 1914. Dad appeared seven years later.

• You could fry eggs on the sidewalk. Speaking of that hotel breakfast I had this morning, . . .

• I saw a man welding without turning on his blowtorch.

• My act is really sizzling!

• It's so hot, we now have only 49 states. Alaska melted!

35. Chicken Crosses the Road

DENA WADE, Autumn's friend since third grade, started this by telling me the basic joke. But it didn't work in Texas or Oregon or England or Saudi Arabia. But with a little local adapting, the Chicken Crossing the Road joke has been one of David Ginn's Greatest Hits. Let me explain—starting with the basic joke.

Why did the chicken cross the road?

Forget all the other answers you've ever heard. This is the best one:

To TEACH the possum IT CAN BE DONE!

In the southeast region of the United States— Georgia, Florida, Tennessee, Kentucky, Alabama, Mississippi, and the Carolinas—this always gets a laugh. Why? Because the possum (or opossum if you're really proper) is the Number One Road Kill Animal on the highways. These nocturnal animals have the tendancy to freeze in automobile and truck headlights while crossing the road at night.

Therefore, autos hit them and leave them in the roadways where we see them the next day. I suppose this is a little morbid, but it's a fact of life. And that fact makes the chicken joke funny because it relates to local real life.

But they don't have possums dead in the roads in the State of Texas, I learned. They have armadillos.

So, why did the chicken cross the road in Texas?

To teach the ARMADILLO it can be done!

That's funny in Texas, New Mexico, Louisiana, lower Mississippi and Alabama, parts of Florida and even some parts of South Georgia, where armadillos have migrated all the way from Texas across the southern panhandle. In South Georgia the farmers call the armadillo a *possum on the half shell.*

But it's not funny in Seattle, Washington, or Portland, Oregon. Up that way they have these huge wormy-like slugs, six inches or longer, that constantly get flattened by trunk tires overnight.

Why did the chicken cross the road in Seattle?

To teach the SLUG it can be done.

They liked that joke in the great Pacific Northwest when I adapted it that way.

But it's not funny in England and Scotland.

They don't have slugs or possums or armadilloes.

But they do have HEDGEHOGS. Yes, same story!

Saudi Arabia?

Would you believe—CAMELS? Yes, where paved highways cross the desert sands, a camel gets hit at least once a week.

They have an unusual law in Saudi Arabia concerning this situation, I've been told. If you hit a camel on the highway at night with your car, it is the fault of the camel's owner (who should have penned up the animal). If you determine who he is, he must pay your damages, plus lose his camel. However, it you hit a camel in the daylight, it is your

fault because you should have seen it, being so big and all. Often, I was also told, if a camel owner finds his camel has been hit at night, he may hurriedly sneak out and cut the tag off the camel's ear so no one can determine the ownership.

So, why did the chicken cross the road in Saudi Arabia?

To teach the CAMEL it can be done!

Note the wording of this punchline: Always the same, just change the animal name. Also note the last three words, delivered with a ONE, TWO,

THREE punch: **CAN BE DONE.** Deliver these last three words dramatically. That helps insure the laugh.

Then, all you have to do is ADAPT. Wherever you go in the world, ask someone before the show: "What is considered roadkill in this part of the country?" People will tell you deer, skunks, possums, raccoons, rabbits, prairie dogs, moose, and a dozen other things. In rural Australia, the answer is kangaroo. Pick the most common animal, insert it into the joke, and use it.

In April 1995 I performed and lectured at the New Zealand Magicians Convention in Wanganui. Just three days before my lecture, I was eating breakfast with Michelle and Alan Watson at their house in Auckland.

I glanced at the local newspaper on the table. There was a half-page story about the problem with a certain animal all over New Zealand, a four-legged furry, nocturnal animal which was destroying farmer's crops. This animal even climbed up into trees to eat out the top new branches and leaves, which in turn destroyed the trees. What was this destructive animal? *A New Zealand possum!*

"Are these possums blinded by auto headlights at night? Do they end up being highway roadkill?" Answer: YES! Unlike our southern American possums, which have thin hairless tails, the New Zealand cousin has a furry tail. But it fit the bill for the joke.

Thus, on the Saturday night convention show, as I finished the Arrowhead routine and before I performed my musical closing, I expressed my thanks and pleasure to all responsible for my return to New Zealand. Then I asked the question:

"Why did the chicken cross the road in Wanganui?"

After a moment's pause, I pulled the trigger.

"To teach the POSSUM **it can be done!**"

The packed Opera House audience laughed not only immediately, but loudly, and suddenly the laughter rolled into applause. Touchdown! All because of a simple joke, a kid riddle, that I had localized successfully.

That's the story. That's the joke. Thank you, Dena Wade. And now, my comedy magic readers, I share it with you . . . a part of this laughter legacy.

36. Trains, Boats, Planes and Automobiles

JOHN CANDY AND STEVE MARTIN made a classic movie titled "Trains, Planes, and Automobiles." It pictures the stress and comedy of travel to the fullest extent.

What's funny about traveling?

Start with the fact that when you arrive at the airport, the first sign you see says TERMINAL. That's scary.

Then you've got to think. Should you, would you, *really* drive an automobile you could purchase with a credit card?

And if my seat cushion can be used for floatation, why didn't I go by boat?

Personally, I love trains. As a kid I rode trains a lot because my father and grandfather worked for the railroad. I loved the way the porter could change our seats into a sleeping berth. That was magic!

All aboard!

• Did you hear about the new car dealer who raffled off a church?

• Speaking of automobiles, my car is so old it has bifocal headlights! I call it Flattery 'cause it gets me nowhere.

Georgia Railroad, @ 1910-15. That's grandfather Fred Ginn, second from the right, an engineer until he retired.

• His car is so old, his licence plate has Roman numerals.

• I don't know much about cars. For years I thought a catalytic converter was a missionary from Rome.

• For a while I was a safe driver, but I gave up it up. Who wants to drive a safe?

• I told him to take a bus home, but he said his wife wouldn't let him keep it.

• Last night I got a puncture in my tire. I didn't see the fork in the road.

• Did you hear about the crazy crook who robbed the train for no reason? He was LOCO with NO MOTIVE!

• How does an engineer remember his way? He has a one track mind.

• How did I learn all about railroading? Simple— I trained myself!

• How do you know when a train goes past? It leaves its tracks. (*Pete McLeod*)

• "All aboard," yelled the conductor, "and if you can't get aboard, get a plank!"

• If your kids want to learn to drive, don't stand in their way.

• As you drive home tonight, watch out for children, especially if they are driving cars.

• A woman driver hit a man and knocked him ten feet into the air. Then she sued him for leaving the scene of the accident.

• I just flew in on a plane so slow they sent the mail ahead by pigeon.

• And remember, folks, if you're driving home tonight, don't forget your car!

• I had to sail across the Atlantic third class. Such a crowd! Fourth class was full.

• I don't know why they put the airport so far out of town. I guess they wanted it near where the planes land.

• Tourists are people who travel thousands of miles to get a picture of themselves standing by their cars.

• I flew in by plane. It would be foolish to try flying any other way.

• I was a little dubious about all these stories of flying saucers. But the other day when I was going down the highway, a large orange object with flashing lights stopped and halted cars on both sides of it. Suddenly a door opened and little people ran out. It was a school bus.

OPPOSITE PAGE: Forget planes, trains, automobiles, and boats. Here is my dad @ 1928 on his steel wheels tricycle. Hey—it worked!

37. Fill-in Remarks

IF IT DIDN'T FIT elsewhere in this book, it's in this chapter! You can plant fill-in remarks any-where in your act, according to the occasion, situation, or audience. Pick your favorites, memorize them, and use them at will.

• I do this for two reasons. The second is the same as the first.

• You may laugh at this, and it would help so much if you did.

• In my opinion, which I hardly ever respect, I think it is true.

• And now if I may, and I see no reason why I mayn't.

• With your permission, or without your per-mission, I'm going to do it anyway.

• I'm here to prove that movies are still your best entertainment.

• Well, the public must be amused.

• This is harder than a cross-eyed puzzle.

• I had this watch fixed, and still it's not right. Here it is twelve o'clock at noon, and the hands point to midnight.

• Ventriloquism is the art by which it is possible to speak through the ears without moving the left eyelid.

• I would much rather borrow a handkerchief than to have somebody lend it to me.

• Take your time and hurry up.

• Does that look strange to you? It doesn't to me.

• I am happy if I can bring a fleeting smile to the lips of a tired shop-girl or a moment of pleasure to a weary book-keeper.

• Welcome to the wonderful land where dreams come true, and things that can't happen really do.

• You may, or may not, believe in predestination, but I think you will be interested in a strange experiment devised to show the extraordinary working of Fate. Throughout the far east, a belief in the working of Fate is all powerful. After all, we are all men of destiny—destined to become or not to become.

• Leave the room, Fred.

• Now we'll go from the ridiculous to the idiotic.

• Follow me and you'll always go wrong.

• You have probably noticed I am a man of few words and much ability.

• Is there no end to this man's capacity?

• Every pose a picture.

Family vacation, summer of 1957. The Ginn family of four, plus two cousins and a best friend. Back Row (L-R): Cousin Vera Plunkett, mom Helen Ginn, dad Frank Ginn. Front row (L-R): sister Nancy Ginn, friend David Hamilton, cousin Barbara Matthews, and a big 11-year-old, David Ginn. Old time photo actually shot in front of the Alamo, San Antonio, Texas. We missed Davy Crockett and Sam Houston by 121 years.

• I was sitting on my porch last night . . . just wishing I had a house to go with it . . . and I thought of this trick.

• I'm making a comeback, which is hard to do because I haven't been anywhere.

• I used to dabble in oils. I ran a gas station.

• Me? In the military? Why, I was classified 4-F by the Boy Scouts!

• You'd never think I used to be a dull person. My idea of a wild time was Coca-Cola and oatmeal cookies. At parties, I stayed in the room with the coats.

• In my opinion, which I respect, . . .

• And now, off to a thundering stop.

• Why didn't I go into the aluminum siding business?

• And now the plot sickens.

• There's one thing about me you must admit. I may not say much, but when I do, it means nothing.

• I'm dying out here—and never left a suicide note.

• *Take fan out of stamped envelope.* Oh, look, FAN MAIL!

• I usually have a ready wit. I just wish it was ready now.

• As a newsboy, I used to sell the *Morning Sun*. The circulation started to drop. How I hated to see the *Morning Sun* go down.

• It's so quiet you could hear a cough drop.

• When I play golf, I always wear two pairs of golfing pants, just in case I get a hole in one.

• This is a funny show. I'm glad I came.

• I would have been a very handsome man, but the nurses changed me in my cradle.

• Even Mason and Dixon had to draw the line somewhere.

• I got a seat in the new stadium. I was up so high I was getting spirit messages. The usher took me halfway up the steps. He said, "You'll have to go the rest of the way yourself. From here on, my nose bleeds." I was the only one in my row without a harp. I turned to a guy and asked, "How do you like the games up here?" He said, "What games? I'm flying the mail to Detroit!"

• My house is made entirely of glass except for the windows—they're made of brick.

• At one time I could speak Spanish and French as well as I could speak English. I was ten months old.

- I love humanity. It's people I don't like.

- Isn't it odd that Washington and Lincoln were both born on holidays?

- Well, we all can't be normal.

- The horn on my car is indifferent. It doesn't give a hoot.

- A spirit appeared and asked, "May I haunt your house?" And I said, "Sure—be my ghost."

- I don't really need these glasses. I just use them for seeing.

- Here's the simple derivation of the word *auditorium:* Audio means to hear. Taurus is bull. So you come to an auditorium to hear . . . uh, nevermind.

- If I say so myself—I doubt it.

- Have you ever got the feeling you're in the wrong business?

- My jokes are works of art. They belong in a museum.

- I have two hands, one on each side. This one is quite all right, but the other hand, on the other hand, sometimes gets left, which isn't right.

- My right hand is exactly nine inches long. Three more inches, and it would have been a foot.

• Two worms in a cemetery were talking things over in dead Ernest.

• I didn't mind going to school. I just didn't like going to classes.

• Do you know the longest word in the dictionary? It's the word SMILES because there's a MILE between the first and last letters.

• You may not like flowers, but eventually they will grow on you.

• Constantly I say to myself: How can one be so clever and work so little?

• I woke up this morning with my eyes wide open. They may have been that way all night. I have no way of knowing.

38. Philosophy

A VERY OLD CHINESE saying states dramatically: *"The peacock cannot speak the same language as the camel, but the beggar who sits cross-legged in winter on the marble steps of the Great Pagoda is nearer to Heaven than the white cockatoo that lays a square egg in the palace of the prince."*

"Night after night," Gene Gordon once told me, "I repeat that ancient Chinese saying . . . in the hope that someday someone will tell me what it means."

Where Gene found this old saying, or whether he wrote it himself, I don't know, nor does it really

matter. I think these words in a nutshell totally sum up the philosophical viewpoint of this entire chapter.
  Go thou now and philosophize.

• Sometimes I feel like more than one person. In fact, my mother showed me a picture of me when I was two. That's when I got double pneumonia.

• Keep in mind that ghost stories are purely seance fiction.

• If you believe that nothing is impossible, try yawning with your mouth closed.

• Eat, drink, and be merry for tomorrow you may lose your credit.

• All men are created equal—but I had to become a magician.

• To err is human. To blame it on someone else is even more human. But to really foul things up requires a computer.

• If you ever get a chance to live your life over again—don't do it.

• The hand is quicker than the eye—that's why you see so many black eyes.

• Belief in miracles was the first religion of the human race. After thousands of years the sorcerers of antiquity became the modern magical entertainers. The magician doesn't pretend supernatural powers, but in entertaining gives back to people the miracles in which they have lost faith.

• Rub-a-Dub-Dub, three men in a tub—come to think of it, that isn't very sanitary, is it?

• Always remember: when things look black, send them to the laundry.

• You can explain that by logic. "If it was so, it might be; and if it were so, it would be; but as it isn't, it ain't." That's the logic of Tweedledee from *Alice in Wonderland.*

• If you step on your automobile brake, are you putting your life in your foot's hands?

• You can accomplish anything if you have patience. You can even carry water in a sieve if you wait until it freezes.

Genuine Rare Photo:

Alfred J. Ginn, my great great grandfather. Born July 2, 1830. Died at age 31 in the U.S. Civil War on October 11, 1861. He is buried in a numbered grave in the Hollywood Cemetery, Richmond, VA.

His wife, Mary Elizabeth Mewborn Ginn, is buried in Bethesda Methodist Church cemetery, a few miles from my home. She and Alfred had four children, including Daddy (Milton) Ginn, and she outlived her husband by 47 years, dying in 1908.

- The best way to make fire with two sticks is to be sure that one of them is a match.

- Imagination is your intelligence having fun.

- The forces of law and order are okay as long as you can lay down the law and give the orders.

- United we stick, divided we're stuck.

- Anybody who thinks he doesn't need a psychiatrist these days should have his head examined.

- Don't give up! Noah was 600 years old before he knew how to build an ark.

- Just remember: A sunset in one land is a sunrise in another. That's a cheerful thought.

- Seems that overnight our world has been made a neighborhood. It still has to be made a brotherhood.

- If we could see ourselves as others see us, the chances are we would deny it.

- You can't weather the storm by storming at the weather.

- The best attitude is KEEP-AT-IT-TUDE.

- It's your attitude, and not your aptitude, that will determine your altitude. *(Thanks, Steve Taylor)*

- Modern psychology tells us that it's bad to be an orphan, terrible to be an only child, damaging to be the youngest, crushing to be in the middle, and a taxing responsibility to be the oldest. There seems no way out except to be born an adult.

• Death is Nature's way of telling you to slow down.

• If a tow truck carries toes, what carries fingers? *(Could the answer be a hand truck?)*

• In the immortal words of Millard Fillmore: "The meek shall inherit the poor."

• If things hadn't of gone like they did—they wouldn't be like they are now. *Pause for effect.* And they were right. *—my father, Frank Ginn*

• You, too, can make somebody happy. Mind your own business.

• Things are sure more like they used to be than they are now.

• A will is a dead give-away.

• No one is entirely useless. Even the worst of us can serve as horrible examples.

• If you stepped on a grape, what would it say? It wouldn't say anything—it would just give a little whine.

• I don't believe in reincarnation, but then I didn't believe in it when I was here before. It may be possible, though. After all, George Washington came back as a bridge. Lincoln as a tunnel. Jefferson as a nickel. I have a friend who made a will and left all his money to himself, just in case.

39. Old Age

YEARS AGO, when cousin Vera Plunkett was in her 70's living in a nursing home, Lynne, Autumn, and I would go visit her sometimes. One day, when Vera's aches and pains were giving her lots of trouble, she remarked to us: "Whatever you do, DON'T EVER GET OLD!"

My first thought was: *How can we help it?*

My second thought: *We have only two choices— get old or die.*

I've often wondered since that day if Cousin Vera was serious or joking. She was a real talker, but I never thought of her as a joker. *Don't ever get old, indeed!* Whatever she meant, my conclusion is that we cannot help getting older, but we can keep our spirits alive with humor and laughter and not GROW OLD.

Even in his last years, when his mind was still lucid, Gene Gordon was still ready with a quip or a pun, either old and tried (but maybe not heard by Lynne or me) or brand new and created straight out of his mind for the occasion.

A lot of the lines which follow sound just like the Gene Gordon we knew. When I read them, I can hear Gene saying them. For me, that makes them more fun! See what you think.

• Anybody can grow old. You just have to live long enough.

• I guess I'm getting old. It takes me twice as long to rest and half as long to get tired. Life not only begins at forty—it begins to show. Nowadays, I get winded playing checkers.

• Middle age is anyone ten years older.

• We cannot help being old, but we can resist being aged.

• I found the secret of youth. Lie about your age.

• Old age is always fifteen years older than you are.

• I'm old enough to have seen the big dipper when it was only a drinking cup.

• It's only a matter of time until every young kid becomes an old goat.

• I'm the darling of the Geritol set.

• When I was your age, I was in love with Shirley Temple. I just got over it last year.

• Cheer up! When you're losing a little on top, you're probably gaining in the middle.

• At my age, this *is* excitement.

• I have a memory like an elephant and a shape to match.

• If I had known I was going to live this long, I'd have taken better care of myself.

• By the time you have learned to make the most of life, most of it is gone!

April 24, 1922. Cousin Vera Plunkett with Daddy Ginn (my great grandfather), Mama (Docia, my great grandmother), aunt Floy Ginn (Emmett's wife), grand uncle Len Ginn and his wife Annie in Lithonia, Georgia. My mom and dad were one year old at the time!

• I'd be 73 next April if it wasn't for one thing—I was born in October.

• We aren't senior citizens. We're drop-outs from the School of Hard Knocks.

• I never feel bad about growing old. Many are denied that privilege.

• I can't tell you how old I am. It keeps changing from minute to minute.

• He's fit as a fizzle and in the punk of condition.

• The remarkable thing about all this is how clever anybody can get in 75 years.

• Excuse my voice—I'm just at the age where its changing.

• How do I know that my youth has been spent? Well, my get up and go has got up and went. But still I can grin when I think where's it's been, and the glorious fun and excitement it meant.

40. Closing Remarks

IF YOU CONCLUDE your performance talking, endeavor to utter something funny, something thoughtful, or something meaningful. In other words, close your performance by causing your audience to laugh, to think, or to leave.

• In closing, may I ask—where would the world be without laughter? Today we found out.

• Saying goodbye after all the fun we've had is very difficult for me. So let me simply bid you farewell in French. I'll just say, "A river of wire." I learned those words in high school French class. The teacher told me it was a romantic way of saying goodbye, but everytime I say it, it still sounds like A RIVER OF WIRE. Well, farewell, and don't let that river of wire rust on you!

• Thank you for saving your applause till the end.

• In closing . . . actually, I'm not through, but I thought I'd give you something to look forward to.

• As you drive home tonight in your expensive cars, keep your eyes open for a rabbit being carried by a friendly hitch hiker—who will be ME.

• Goodbye, friends. Say, does anyone know what time the midnight flight leaves? Sixty minutes past eleven? Sixty minutes till one? Gee, I thought that flight left on the runway! *(Thanks, Abb!)*

• Let me say this in leaving you: Remember, it's not the soup that sloshes out of the bowl when you're in a hurricane on the high sea that is all important—it is the ABC's of the alphabet soup of life. Catch them with your spoon of opportunity before they slip past your reach and spell DISASTER.

• When you get home tonight and tuck yourself in bed—remember that for these few moments we were together, and I was your only magician.

• In closing, I would like to say . . . that of all the audiences I have ever spent entertaining, you— Ladies and Gentlemen—are . . . without a doubt . . . the most recent.

• As we wrap up this frivolity, let me quote an old Chinese proverb: *If so desired, you will meet each other; if not, you will miss each other.* Tonight we have had the privelege to meet and enjoy each other, and tomorrow I will miss each and every one of you. So until I see you again, remember this other old Chinese proverb: *Think twice—and say nothing!*

• Now it's time . . . to say goodbye . . . to all the family . . . M-I-C-K-E-Y M-O-U-S-E! Oops! Wrong show!

• Remember—
If you sleep on your back, you can study the ceiling.
If you sleep on your side, you can study the wall.
If you sleep on your front, you can study your pillow.
But if you're really asleep, you can't study at all!

• Your good taste in applauding my silly efforts has certainly been appreciated by me.

June, 1927. My dad Frank Ginn at age six pretending to be a blind beggar boy at the old home place in Lithonia, Georgia.

Observe the sox falling down, wrinkled shorts, long sleeved shirt, and tossled hair.

Isn't this what college students are wearing in the 1990's?

• There is a time for seriousness and a time for fun. I hope during the show you have seriously had a lot of fun, for I seriously planned it to be that way.

• Laughter and applause are music to my ears, and tonight you have written me a concerto. I thank you from my heart. Goodnight!

• Well, folks, you've been an absolutely smashing audience. In fact, that one fellow over there has smashed a dozen mosquitoes while I've been on stage.

• If you would like to show me a token of your appreciation when the show is over—for the fun time we've had together—before you go out, just leave me an imprint of your MasterCard or VISA.

• Thank you, Ladies and Gentlemen, for allowing me to stand here before you. And I deeply appreciate you standing behind me during the performance, even though you were sitting in front of me.

• I'm sorry to say that now it is time for me to say that I must say goodbye. It's an old saying, but as sayings go I feel it says the truth, that "be it said that anyone could say one good thing about what you have said, he should say it now or forever hold his say," if you see what I'm saying. Well, I've said enough. Thank you! Say goodnight! *Goodnight!* Well, I'll say! You don't say! Goodnight to you, too!

No End to the Laughter

HERB OUTLAW, our family minister for nine years, has a favorite cliche, which he uses when people are thinking in the wrong direction. Herb says they're "putting the *em-FAH-sis* on the wrong *sy-LLA-ble.*"

During my formative years in magic, from age 12-20, my concept was to trick and fool the audience. I was putting the *em-FAH-sis on the wrong si-LLA-ble.*

Thanks to my English mentor, Harold Taylor, I changed my direction. According to Harold, the most important thing in a show is to *entertain* the audience, regardless of whether, as a magician, you fool them.

This is not to say you cannot baffle the spectators with magic illusions. But it clearly indicates that *entertainment comes first.*

In the English-speaking world, the clever use of words always plays well. The performer who can make people forget themselves through laughter—*especially good clean laughter*—will always be well-received. As Fetaque Sanders often said, "Patter packs better than props." Mix those words *with* your props and *voila—comedy magic!*

In closing these pages, I encourage you to try this material and use that which suits the performer in you. We each are a little different. We should be. So each of you will need to decide within *what is* and *what is not* the funny side of you.

There are no pat answers. If you can't decide alone, try the material on friends or audiences to see what happens. If it fails, toss it out or try again. If it succeeds, run with it.

Steve Smith, former director of Ringling Brothers Barnum & Bailey Clown College, put it in a nutshell at a talk he gave: "Society needs a release valve. Humor—*yes, LAUGHTER*—**is** that release valve."

Let there always be laughter. Hear it in your heart, then translate that to your audiences. *Laughter.* I am beginning to think it is more important than any of the tricks. Perhaps, indeed, *laughter is the real magic.*

Do you love rabbits? I do. Real live rabbits and toy stuffed bunnies, too. Most people do. Therefore, what I am about to share with you may touch a delicate nerve, especially if you have performed with your own little "Harvey" over a period of time.

Several years ago, up in the North Georgia mountains, school custodian Paul Batson helped me load up my props after a performance. At the back of the van, Paul admired my rabbit.

"My friend Bill's wife had a pet rabbit," he told me. "But something happened to it not long ago."

I had heard these "rabbit horror stories" before, usually told to me by kids who had lost their pet bunnies, one way or another. However, I listened out of courtesy.

"A few weeks ago Bill worked late on a Friday night and came home real tired," explained Paul. "He told his wife to let him sleep a while the next morning and not wake him up.

"Well, next morning he crawled out of bed about ten o'clock, pulled on his pants and a T-shirt, and headed for the kitchen. He found coffee still warm and a note from his wife, saying she'd got up early and went to the store and would be back home in a few hours.

"So Bill took his morning coffee out on the back porch and sat down in a rocking chair. They live up on a mountain about five miles from here and have a real nice view.

"There he sat, enjoying the morning November air, when up trots Bill's hunting dog he calls Rex. And Rex had this white rabbit, covered with blood and dirt, in his teeth."

"Was the rabbit dead?" I asked.

"Yes," the fellow told me, "dead as a doornail. Not only that, it was Bill's wife's pet rabbit. She called it Fluffy. Kept it in a cage out in the trees behind the house to keep it cool. Had the thing for five years and just loved it.

"Well, Bill about had a heart attack. It was no mistaking the rabbit in the dog's mouth. It was Fluffy. Bill knew it by the markings.

"He said, 'Rex, man, what have you done! Margaret is gonna kill you for this, and then she'll kill me. We gotta do something.'

"So Bill got the water hose and washed the dirt and blood off the dead rabbit. Next he went in the house and got a hair dryer, you know, one of those blow-dryers, and he dried the rabbit off real good. Then he and Rex took the dead rabbit down to the cage and locked it back inside.

"A while later, while Bill was taking a shower, his wife came home. She unloaded a few things, told him she was home, then said she had to go check on Fluffy.

"Bill cringed when he heard that. *Here it comes,* he thought. A few minutes later as he was getting dressed, Bill heard Margaret yelling, 'Bill! Bill! Hurry, come quick!'

"So Bill hurried out there into the yard where Margaret was standing. She motioned for him to follow and said, 'It's Fluffy!' So down she goes to the rabbit cage with Bill trottin' behind her.

"She pointed at the cage. 'Look in there!' she said. So Bill looked, and there was the rabbit right where he'd put it.

"'Oh, I'm sorry,' he said, 'looks like he died.'

"Margaret looked at Bill and said, 'I *know* he died, Bill. He's been acting sluggish for two days. This morning at 7:30 I found him dead in his cage, and I buried him right over there in that fresh dirt. Now he's out of the grave, cleaned up like he's going to church, and back in his cage! If the Good Lord was gonna resurrect him, the least He could have done was bring Fluffy back *alive!*'"

The next time you step out on stage, make sure your audience knows you're alive.

Make sure they are having fun through what you do and say. Make them smile, make them grin, make them laugh. Make them forget what's wrong with the world while they get caught up in what's funny and happy.

Leave them with your own laughter legacy . . . so that maybe, just maybe, they will remember you.

Index

Sunday School, 1952. Back row. Who's the only kid wearing a red and black cowboy shirt? You guessed it—me!

The David Ginn Book List

1. Colorful Magic (1969)
2. Strictly Visuals (1970)
3. The Snake Can (1970)
4. Fantasio Cane Book No. 1 '71
5. The Quick-Change Silk '71
6. Magic That Moves Me (1971)
7. The Magic 13 (1972)
8. New Dove Magic (1972)
9. Fantasio Cane Book No. 2 '73
10. Strictly Visuals Two (1973)
11. Close-Up A-Ginn (1974)
12. Comedy Cut & Restored Neckerchief (1974)
13. Comedy Linking Rings '74
14. Comedy Card on Back (1974)
15. Comedy Warm-ups for Children's Shows (1975)
16. 33 Easy Magic Tricks (1975)
17. Comedy Lunch Box (1975)
18. Bringing Home Laughs '76
19. Professional Magic for Children (1976)
20. Starting in Magic (1976)
21. Matchbox Delights (1977)
22. Little Black Book (1977)
23. Fantasio Book No. 3 (1978)
24. Children Laugh Louder '78
25. Promoting Me and You I '79
26. Sure-Fire Magic (1979)
27. Keep It A Secret! (1980)
27-A **Gene Gordon's Magical Legacy (1980) Ed/Pub**
28. Colorful Magic: Twelve Years Later (1980)
29. Feather Flowers from Nowhere (1981)
30. Fantasio Book No. 4 (1981)
31. 50 Ways to Make Children Laugh (1981)
32. Super Math Puzzles (1981)
33. Kidbiz (1982)
34. Fantasio Book No. 5 (1982)
35. Fantasio 6: The Color Changing Lighter (1982)
36. School Show Presentation, Vol. 1 (1983) audio/book
37. Promoting Me and You II '83
38. Straight Talk about Ent.ertaining Children (1983) audio
39. Magic and Monsters for Kids I Love (1984)
40. School Show Presentation, Vol. 2-3 (1985) audio/book
40-A **The Comedy Magic Textbook (1986) Ed/Pub**
41. Almost Unpublished (1987)
42. Money Math Magic (1987)
43. Live Kidbiz (1988) VIDEO
44. Nearly Unpublished (1989)
45. It's About Time (1990) video
46. Kidshow List of Lists (1990)
47. Behind the Scenes '91 video
47-A **Safety Magic for Children (1991) Ed/Pub.**
48. Visuelle Zauberkunst (Germany 1991)
49. Comedy Magic Catalog
50. Bag of Magic (1992) video
51. Clown Magic (1993)
52. Lost and Found Magic Lecture (1993) audio
53. Partly Unpublished (1993)
54. Magic They Love to See (1994) video
55. Live Kidbiz 3: Costuming Kids for Laughs (1995) video
56. Live Kidbiz 4: Storytelling with Magic (1995) video
57. Komedy Kid-Show Kassettes (1995) 3 audios with Sammy Smith & Steve Taylor
58. The Only Three Ways to Book Your Show (1996)
59. Magic of Hawaii (1997) video
60. Laughter Legacy (1998)